THE ROYAL HORTICULTURAL SOCIETY
PRACTICAL GUIDES

PLANTS
FOR SHADE

THE ROYAL HORTICULTURAL SOCIETY
PRACTICAL GUIDES

PLANTS
FOR SHADE

LINDEN HAWTHORNE

DORLING KINDERSLEY
LONDON • NEW YORK • SYDNEY • MOSCOW
www.dk.com

LONDON, NEW YORK, MUNICH, MELBOURNE, DELHI

PRODUCED FOR DORLING KINDERSLEY BY PAGEONE,
Cairn House, Elgiva Lane, Chesham, Buckinghamshire

PROJECT EDITOR Charlotte Stock

SERIES EDITOR Pamela Brown
SERIES ART EDITOR Stephen Josland

MANAGING EDITOR Louise Abbott
MANAGING ART EDITOR Lee Griffiths

First published in Great Britain in 1999
Reprinted 2002
by Dorling Kindersley Limited,
80 Strand, London WC2R 0RL

A Penguin Company

A CIP catalogue for this book is available from the British Library.
ISBN 0 7513 47221

Reproduced by Colourscan, Singapore
Printed and bound by Star Standard Industries, Singapore

See our complete catalogue at
www.dk.com

CONTENTS

GARDENING IN SHADE

ADVANTAGES OF SHADE

IF SHADE DID NOT OCCUR naturally in a garden, it would become necessary to create some – simply because shade is essential to get the best from so many exquisite garden plants. Shade is indispensable in providing interesting planting opportunities and, indeed, it becomes a positive necessity in warm climates.

A WEALTH OF SHADE-LOVERS

Since the range of plants that thrive in shade is immense, gardeners seldom need to feel restricted by the lack of suitable material for growing in shady sites. While there are relatively few shade-loving annuals and grasses, and virtually no water plants, woods and forests have provided a wealth of bulbs, perennials, ferns and woody plants that can be grown in shady gardens. Such diverse plant types provide unlimited opportunities for the creation of mixed plantings that ensure colour and interest throughout the year.

◄WOODLAND NATIVES *Where space is limited, ferns, ivies and violas can be grown in containers, creating beautiful textural compositions in shady corners. Keep steps and paths clear of moss and algae, which thrive in shade and make conditions dangerous underfoot.*

◄COOL SHADE *A cool, shady niche maintains the lush, verdant foliage of ferns and hostas.*

THE BENEFITS OF SHADE

Shady areas in the garden actually increase the range of plants that may be grown successfully. Many natives of forests and woods need shade of some sort; in fact, they are likely to scorch or fail in sunny,

---

A shady site protects plants against extremes of temperature

---

open sites. They usually flower better in shade, and their flowers and foliage stay fresh for longer periods.

In a shaded site, it is easy to provide the cool, moist conditions needed by many spring-flowering plants, such as snowdrops, winter aconites and hellebores, during the summer. Cooler and more humid than an open site, a shady bed is less exposed to

SUN PROTECTION FOR PLANTS
Shade-loving plants such as sweet woodruff
(Galium odoratum) *need protection from the hottest sun if they are not to suffer from sun scorch in summer, especially in warm climates.*

TYPES OF SHADE

- LIGHT shade is cast by buildings, walls or fences onto sites that are open to the sky.
- DAPPLED shade is cast by the canopy of deciduous trees when in full leaf.
- PARTIAL shade is temporary and moves with the sun's passage through the sky.
- DEEP shade occurs beneath evergreen trees or in sunless alleys between tall buildings.

extremes of temperature in summer and winter and, depending on the type of shade, it may be better able to retain soil moisture. Shade reduces the need for watering, and it ensures that plants look lush and verdant in mid- to late summer, when those in sun may be past their best.

Sunless sites may be cold during the winter months, but their low temperatures help to discourage dormant plants from emerging too early where spring frosts could be dangerous. Frozen plants will defrost slowly in shade, avoiding the damage caused by rapid thawing in sun.

Damp shade does attract slugs and snails, but mites, aphids and other pests proliferate more freely in sunny conditions.

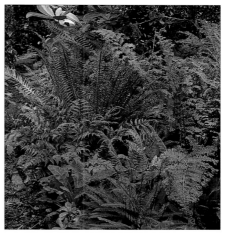

▲ MOISTURE IN THE AIR
*Cool, humid shade in a site that is sheltered
from warm, drying summer winds makes
an ideal environment for ferns.*

◀ RETAINING MOISTURE
*Light shade shields soil from direct sun to
help meet the needs of moisture-loving plants.*

DESIGN CONSIDERATIONS

The colour palette formed by shade-
loving plants lends itself to the creation
of subtle planting schemes that combine
a hundred shades of blue, grey, green and
gold. Foliage forms and surface textures
that contrast and harmonize invariably
outlast the flowering period of shade-
loving plants and can be woven into
a design to help ensure a prolonged
season of interest in the garden.

While themes that rely on variations
in plant shape and habit may, at first,
seem less dramatic than highly coloured
plants in bright sun, they can be just
as satisfying and are certainly no less
beautiful. Shade-loving plants range in
height from low-growing ground cover,
such as sweet woodruff (*Galium*) to
the showy grandeur of rhododendrons,
lending themselves to layered, flowing
compositions with strong focal points
and a sense of perspective.

The hot, dazzling colours that are typically
associated with many sun-loving plants
are not so common in the blooms of shade-
bearers, many of which are endowed with
a soft spectrum of mostly pastel colours
that bring cool luminosity to even the
darkest spot. The effectiveness of this type
of planting can be enhanced by the use of
foliage plants (*see pp.14–15*) whose leaves
are marbled, striped or splashed in shades
of white, cream and gold.

OVERHANGING BRANCHES

If a neighbour's tree casts undesirable
shade across your garden, first try friendly
consultation with the owner to obtain his
or her permission to cut back the offending
branches. Should this approach fail, the law
allows you to prune back to a line drawn
vertically upwards from the boundary of
your property. The prunings are considered
to be your neighbour's property, so return or
dispose of them with the owner's permission.

Types of Shade

THE SHADE IN YOUR GARDEN will often prove to be a combination of several shade types that vary in duration. Shade changes throughout each day as the sun crosses the sky, and by season because the trajectory of the winter sun is lower – markedly so at high latitudes – than that of summer. An understanding of the particular shade type, and its permanence and density, is invaluable when choosing plants that thrive in the light conditions of any given garden site.

Light and Dappled Shade

The two easiest shade conditions in which to raise plants are light and dappled shade. Even plants that are normally grown in sun may thrive in these types of shade, although they can become leggy as their stems grow tall in search of light.

Light shade is the type of permanent shade that is cast by a building or wall on sites that are otherwise open to the sky. It also occurs at woodland edges or at the margins of a tree canopy. The overall effect of light shade is most marked in winter, when plants are dormant or quiescent, but it is reduced merely to the absence of direct sunlight in the growing season, when the sun is higher in the sky.

This type of shade is a positive advantage in warm climates, where the combination of sun and shelter can raise summer temperatures excessively.

Shade that occurs beneath deciduous vegetation will be dappled, forming a moving patchwork of varying intensities of shade that changes with the sun's daily course. Seasonal variations tend to be dramatic, with pronounced shade when trees are in full leaf, but less marked effects when low winter light slants beneath the trees or through a canopy of open branches. Many spring-flowering plants have adapted to this regime, and complete their flowering season before the canopy closes over and reduces the light.

PROVIDING A
SUN SCREEN
*Light shade at
the margins of an
overhead canopy
provides ideal
conditions for plants
like busy Lizzies
(Impatiens) that
may scorch and
fade in direct sun.*

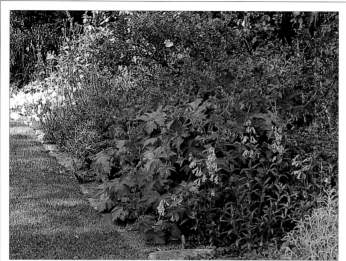

PARTIAL SHADE

As the sun moves across the sky, a site with partial or part-day shade may receive between two and six hours of direct sun daily. This situation is ideal for plants that tolerate sun but little shade. In fact, only the most committed sun-loving plants fail to thrive in such conditions. The distinct advantage of partial shade is that it may alleviate the burning effects of mid-day or afternoon sun. This protection from scorch is most desirable at low latitudes;

> Many spring-flowering plants bloom before the tree canopy closes over

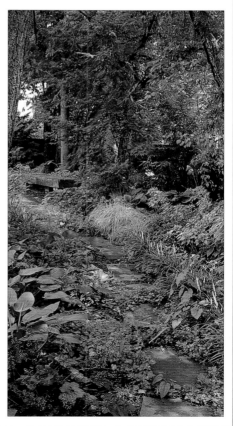

the sun's heat and light become more intense the nearer the equator. Even in cool climates, you should not overlook the value of afternoon shade in your garden during high summer. Morning shade maintains the cool night-time air that is enjoyed by shade-loving plants, but if it is succeeded by direct afternoon sun, these plants can be subjected to an extreme rise in temperature with which few of them are able to cope.

DEEP SHADE

This type of shade occurs beneath dense, evergreen trees or shrubs, at the base of high walls, or in passageways that run between tall buildings, and may be near-permanent if little or no direct sunlight strikes the site. Where plants are grown in the deep shade cast by trees or shrub cover, they may also need to cope with poor, dry soil (*see facing page*).

A planting scheme in deep shade needs more thoughtful planning than those in lighter types of shade, but there are several ways to help improve the planting conditions. First, the plants selected need to be shade-demanding, rather than simply shade-tolerant. These are plants that, in nature, inhabit the woodland floor or other shady niches. The soil in a deciduous or mixed woodland tends to be rich in organic

matter, thanks to the annual leaf fall, and is, consequently, well-aerated and moisture-retentive. Mimic these conditions by adding organic matter to the soil when planting (*see p.48*) and by applying a layer of mulch (*see p.50*) annually in spring. Site plants at least 45cm away from the base of walls to lessen the effects of rain shadow – an area of sheltered ground that receives less rain than an open site.

> A thick organic mulch
> in spring helps to
> alleviate dry conditions

You can increase ambient light levels by painting surrounding walls with light-reflective colours, and by using mirrors and pale-coloured paving or gravel. An unplanted water feature (aquatic plants need sun), especially one where water is constantly moving, such as a bubble or wall fountain, will also contribute a little sparkle and reflect light in a shady site.

PLANTING BENEATH A CANOPY
This varied planting lightens up an area of moist soil shaded by trees in full leaf. In the foreground, variegated irises thrive in the higher light levels bordering the canopy.

DRY SHADE

The most difficult garden situation for gardeners and plants alike is that of dry shade, which occurs in the rain shadow of walls and beneath the canopy of dense or evergreen foliage, especially where shallow-rooting trees and shrubs are taking all the moisture. The cool, sheltered conditions found in most shady sites reduce moisture loss from the soil and leaf surfaces, but if rain shadows are present, then the soil cannot be fully replenished by rainfall. The bold foliage produced by many shade-loving plants to maximize the available light contributes to the problem, since more water is lost from large leaves.

Relatively few plants are able to thrive in dry shade, which restricts the scope of planting schemes, so it really helps to improve the dry soil. Add organic matter at planting time, and apply a moisture-retentive mulch to damp soil in early spring each year. Where shallow roots cause dry conditions, you can line planting holes with a perforated sheet of plastic to conserve moisture in the short term.

▲THRIVING DAMP
Damp shade provides an ideal site for Ajuga reptans *and* Cardamine pratensis, *which occur naturally in damp shady niches.*

▼TESTING THE LIMITS
While it is one of the most problematical of sites, deep, dry shade is tolerated by a small range of plants, including useful ground-cover perennials such as this comfrey.

FOLIAGE PLANTS FOR SHADE

PLANTING SCHEMES that make the most of the subtle variations in form, texture and colour of foliage are the mainstays of shade gardening. Foliage offers interest throughout the growing season – year-round for evergreens – and the beauties of foliage can easily equal the often short-lived interest of flowers. Foliage plants can prove useful as well as beautiful when used as weed-smothering ground cover or, as with variegated plants, if used to brighten shady corners.

FORM AND FUNCTION

The diverse sizes, forms and textures that make the foliage of shade-loving plants so satisfying provide an increased leaf-surface area that allows the plants to make the most of the low levels of available light. For example, many ferns have numerous

Spreading foliage and large leaves capture the most light

tiny, divided leaflets, while hostas produce broad, flat leaves. Each leaf borne on the arching stems of Solomon's seal (*Polygonatum*) is positioned at an angle where it can receive maximum sunlight.

▲ FOLIAGE GROUND COVER
Here, the variegated form of ground elder (Aegopodium podagraria) *provides a light-reflecting carpet beneath bluebells in dappled shade.*

◀ LAYERED EFFECTS
The coarse leaves of comfrey contrast attractively with those of variegated elder (Sambucus), *while honeysuckle lends height to the scheme.*

▲ ATTRACTIVE ASSOCIATIONS
Even plants grown primarily for their blooms (here, Geranium tuberosum *and* Tulipa greigii) *can form pleasing foliage compositions that provide interest after the plants have flowered.*

◀ CONTRASTING FORM AND TEXTURE
Shade-loving foliage plants offer a variety of form, colour and variegation that can make the perfect foil for other textures in a shady border or container garden in a courtyard.

COLOURED FOLIAGE

Splashes, spots and marbling in tints of white, cream or gold are invaluable for providing highlights in shade; pale colours can appear almost luminous. Bear in mind, though, that variegated areas on a leaf lack chlorophyll, the green pigment plants use as part of the food-making process to capture energy from sunlight. The reduced area of green in the leaves makes variegated plants less vigorous than their all-green counterparts. As a result, many variegated plants, especially ivies (*Hedera*), lose their variegation in deep shade and their leaves revert to all green. The reduced vigour of variegated plants can be a positive advantage in the garden, especially if their green-leaved counterparts are known to be rampant, as with ground elder and periwinkle.

LEAF INTEREST FOR SHADE

EVERGREEN FOLIAGE

Ajuga reptans
Bergenia many
Broom *(Ruscus)*
Christmas box *(Sarcococca)*
Euphorbia amygdaloides var. *robbiae*
Ferns most
Ivies *(Hedera helix)*
Holly *(Ilex)* many
Pachysandra terminalis
Periwinkle *(Vinca)* most
Firethorn *(Pyracantha)*
Violets *(Viola odorata)*

VARIEGATED FOLIAGE

Light to moderate shade

Cyclamen hederifolium, Euonymus fortunei cultivars, *Hedera helix* many, *Hosta* many

Moderate shade

Convallaria majalis 'Albostriata', *Lunaria annua* 'Variegata', *Polygonatum* x *hybridum* 'Striatum', *Tolmiea menziesii* 'Taff's Gold'

Moderate to deep shade

Ajuga reptans cultivars, *Asarum hartwegii, Aucuba japonica, Brunnera macrophylla, Fatsia japonica, Lamium*

Flowering Plants for Shade

Plants that flower well in shade offer a subtle colour palette that comprises luminous shades of yellow, white, cream, pale pinks and purples, and cool blues. This range of colours is shown off at its well-preserved best when protected from the bleaching effects of the sun and is much enhanced where the soft hues appear to glow against a lush backdrop of sumptuous, shade-loving foliage accompanied by cool, still air that may be perfumed by fragrant flowers.

Mixed Plantings

Planning mixed schemes to make the most of a range of ornamental features for each season is essential for year-round interest. The most successful flowering plants for shady sites are those that occur naturally in shade, along with the cultivars bred or selected from these species. Shade-lovers usually bloom between late winter and early summer, before the tree canopy closes over. Light levels reduce dramatically once the trees are in leaf, so plants that produce

> Many natives of woodland and forest flower in spring

flowers later in the year, or those that offer attractive fruits, fine foliage or autumn colour, become all the more valuable.

A MIX OF ORNAMENTAL FEATURES
Ajugas provide a mantle of colour between spring and early summer. The foliage later provides a ground-covering foil for the elegant leaves and summer flowers of hostas.

▲ SPRING-FLOWERING WOODLANDERS
The deeply coloured flowers of forget-me-nots and pulmonarias make a glorious association in a woodland setting in spring.

◄ EXTENDING THE SEASON OF INTEREST
As bluebells and trilliums fade, Rodgersia aesculifolia, *with its architectural foliage and spires of summer flowers, comes into its own.*

PROLONGING FLOWERING

Plants that are truly shade-demanding invariably bloom well and for long periods in shade, whereas those that merely tolerate shade may prove reluctant to bloom in low levels of light. Annuals and rapid-growing climbers, in particular, are often more successful when given an application of a balanced, slow-release fertilizer in spring. If the flowers are still sparse, however, a high-potash fertilizer such as tomato feed, applied at the manufacturer's recommended rate, helps to encourage the production of flowers.

PLANTS WITH ADDED VALUE

LONG-LASTING FLOWERS

Japanese anemones *(Anemone* x *hybrida)*
Begonia semperflorens, B. coccinea
Foxgloves *(Digitalis)*
Hostas most
Busy Lizzies *(Impatiens)*
Lamium most
Lonicera periclymenum
Welsh poppy *(Meconopsis cambrica)*
Tobacco plants *(Nicotiana sylvestris,*
 N. x *sanderae* cultivars, **N. 'Lime Green')**
Jacob's ladder *(Polemonium)*

SEVERAL SEASONS OF INTEREST

Arum italicum Spring flowers, good winter foliage, orange berries in autumn.
Astilbes Fine foliage, summer flowers, dry flowerheads through autumn and winter.
Cyclamen hederifolium Autumn flowers, good winter ground cover, marbled leaves.
Hostas Excellent foliage, good ground cover, with fragrant, mid- to late summer flowers.
Liriope muscari Evergreen, good ground cover, autumn flowers, tolerant of dry shade.
Pyracantha Evergreen foliage, spring flowers, colourful, winter-persistent berries.

PLANTS FOR SPRING

A S THE DAYS LENGTHEN with the onset of spring, anticipation in the shade garden increases as new buds break to reveal the lush greens and bright tints of emergent foliage – especially so with the unfurling croziers of ferns, which are often beautifully shaded in tones of pink or chestnut-brown. Spring-flowering perennials, bulbs and shrubs add highlights of jewel-bright colours, first to bare earth and branches and later, as spring progresses, to the textures and hues of foliage.

PLANNING AHEAD

Spring is undoubtedly the easiest season to plan for. Given the range of suitable plants, it can be difficult to resist filling a site entirely with spring-flowering species, leaving little space for plants that are at their best later in the year. In gardens with acid soil, the temptation to mass camellias and rhododendrons together, where space permits, is particularly hard to resist. To avoid inadvertently creating gaps or dull areas in your planting scheme as spring plants fade, be sure to site spring-flowering plants among others that will take their place as the seasons progress.

SPRING COLOURS
Daffodils add colour to a mantle of fresh epimedium leaves that come into their own glory a little later in the season.

CATCHING THE
EARLY LIGHT
*In dappled shade
beneath deciduous
trees, spring-flowering
bulbs such as
the trout lily*
(Erythronium
revolutum) *provide
colour before the
canopy closes over
and reduces the light.*

PLANT AND PROTECT

Few sights are more glorious in early spring than carpets of snowdrops, winter aconites or anemones. The most pleasing effects can be achieved if bulbs and perennials are planted in loose drifts. Do this by scattering bulbs randomly, and planting them where they fall. Similarly,

> Use naturalistic drifts
> to copy the way that
> plants grow in the wild

group perennials in odd numbers of, say, three, five or seven, taking care to avoid block plantings of geometric shapes. Autumn is the time to plant spring bulbs and, to get the best effect from your spring display, site them where the dappled sunlight strikes the earth in autumn.

Spring signals the emergence of slugs and snails – a shade plant's worst enemies. Take action to reduce populations (*see p.52*) and opt for plants that have a good resistance to these pests (*see p.21*).

GOOD ASSOCIATIONS

EARLY SPRING BULBS
Anemone blanda
Winter aconites (*Eranthis hyemalis*)
Snowdrops (*Galanthus*)

EARLY SPRING PERENNIALS
Wood anemones (*Anemone nemorosa*)
Bergenias
Hellebores (*Helleborus*)
Primroses (*Primula vulgaris*)
Lungworts (*Pulmonaria*)

MID- TO LATE SPRING BULBS
Arum italicum 'Marmoratum'
Erythroniums most
Bluebells (*Hyacinthoides*)
Squills (*Scilla siberica*)
Spring snowflake (*Leucojum vernum*)
Ornithogalums

MID- TO LATE SPRING PERENNIALS
Brunneras
Chelidonium majus 'Flore Pleno'
Epimediums
Geranium phaeum
Lamium maculatum
Trilliums

Plants for Summer

Once the spring flowers are over, companion summer plants begin to assume their full beauty in the cool, moist, equable conditions that shade can provide. Most of these will be plants grown for their foliage, set out to display their own individual attractions as well as to provide a lush backdrop to the precious summer jewels of those plants that do flower through the summer months. Careful selection – and a little manipulation – will make the most of their display.

Repaying your Choice

Compared with the numerous shade-loving plants that flower in spring, the choice of summer-flowering species is limited. Try to choose plants that are noted for their long blooming period or that offer good value during the summer. *Clematis tangutica* produces plenty of bright yellow flowers over mid- to late summer, followed by fluffy seedheads that extend interest beyond the flowering period. In terms of foliage, ferns provide many months of beauty, from the unfurling croziers in mid-spring to the play of light on their graceful fronds through summer. Hostas also offer long seasons of foliage, while some perennials, annuals and biennials more than repay time spent in their selection and placement. Many tobacco plants (*Nicotiana*), some of which carry an evening scent, and Japanese anemones (*Anemone* x *hybrida*) are valued for their long flowering periods in summer.

SUMMER INTEREST
Ferns (here Dryopteris) *and* Hosta fortunei *var.* aureomarginata *look good from early summer. The foliage is enhanced by the hosta's mid-summer spires of mauve bells.*

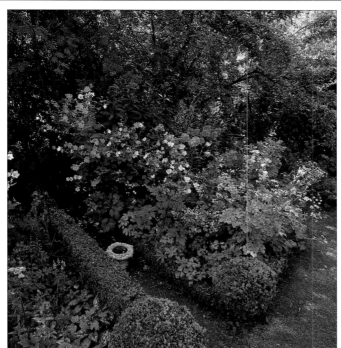

ONGOING BLOOMS
This grouping of
Japanese anemones
(Anemone × hybrida),
astrantias and
lavatera will provide
a display of flowers
over many months
in summer.

ENCOURAGING THE DISPLAY

Several techniques can prolong a flowering display in shade. Deadheading encourages more flowers in most plants, especially if it is followed by an application of balanced fertilizer. Many shade-loving hardy annuals can be sown in autumn or spring, so that the autumn-sown seeds flower in early summer, and will be followed on by the spring sowings. Biennials, such as foxgloves, flower in early summer if sown in late spring in the previous year, but they may bloom later the same year if sown under glass in late winter or early spring.

VALUABLE PLANTS FOR SUMMER

GOOD FOLIAGE

Ajuga reptans
Alchemilla most
Astilbes
Ferns most
Hostas most
Kirengeshoma palmata
Lamiums
Rodgersias
Shortia galacifolia
Vancouveria hexandra
Periwinkles (*Vinca*)

SLUG-RESISTANT PLANTS

Actaea
Astilbes most
Begonia grandis subsp. *evansiana*
Brunnera macrophylla
Bugles (*Ajuga*)
Foxgloves (*Digitalis*) most
Epimediums
Hellebores (*Helleborus*)
Jacob's ladder (*Polemonium*)
Monkshood (*Aconitum*)
Sweet woodruff (*Galium odoratum*)

AUTUMN AND WINTER INTEREST

As SUMMER TURNS to autumn, there are fewer flowers to be had, and attention turns to other ornamental features to decorate the garden. In autumn, plants with good foliage colour assume great importance, and fruits, berries and dry seedheads come into their own, many persisting into winter and looking most striking when rimed with hoar frost. In winter, the stark outlines of leafless trees and shrubs stand out in anticipation of the first of the new season's spring bulbs.

MAKING AUTUMN GLOW

As the growing season comes to a close, the few plants that offer autumn flowers in shade are all the more valued and deserve to be given prominence. The swathes of colour created by *Cyclamen hederifolium* are followed by silver-marbled leaves that make a dense carpet even in dry soil. Position *Iris foetidissima* where its glossy, bright-orange seeds can be seen at close quarters, perhaps offset by the tight violet-mauve flower spikes of *Liriope muscari* – both thrive in dry shade. Leave the dry seedheads of astilbes and honesty to enhance your autumn display, together with colourful grasses such as *Hakonechloa macra* 'Aureola'. Many berrying plants are at their best in autumn, from the orange spikes of arums and red-fruited actaeas to

> ### Take advantage of seedheads, berries and good autumn colour

the arching branches of cotoneasters and pyracanthas. Set these plants against the autumn foliage provided by *Amelanchier, Enkianthus, Fothergilla* and witch hazel.

► AUTUMN CAMEO
The heavily veined leaves of Rodgersia pinnata *turn to warm shades of red and brown in autumn.*

▼ STRIKING SPIKES
The violet-mauve spikes of lilyturf (Liriope muscari) *introduce color in areas of dry shade.*

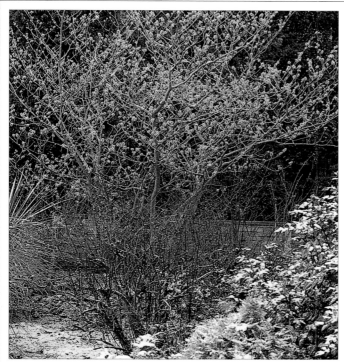

WINTER GOLD
The elegant, vase-shaped branch framework of witch hazel (Hamamelis) *is spangled with spidery yellow flowers in late winter, making it an ideal companion for late winter bulbs.*

LASTING THROUGH WINTER

During the dull winter months, interest in the shady garden is maintained by winter-persistent berries on shrubs and trees and the dry seedheads of perennials and grasses that have been left in place during the autumn clear-up. Some of the ferns, such as *Onoclea sensibilis* and *Osmunda regalis*, will continue to display their dark, fertile fronds, while evergreens, such as the variegated forms of *Aucuba japonica* and *Euonymus fortunei*, will offer gleams of colour in the winter landscape.

The stark architectural outlines of bare branches in shrubs such as *Aralia* and *Hamamelis* are at their elegant best in winter. Their open branchwork lets through valuable light for drifts of winter aconites or snowdrops (*Galanthus*), the late winter bulbs that herald the return of spring and signal a new beginning to the cycle of the seasons.

LATE-SEASON INTEREST

AUTUMN FLOWERS

Cimicifuga simplex
Gentiana asclepiadea
Hydrangea paniculata, H. quercifolia, H. serrata
Kirengeshoma palmata
Liriope muscari
Tricyrtis formosana, T. hirta

AUTUMN AND WINTER FRUITS

Callicarpa bodinieri
Hollies (*Ilex*)
Skimmia
Snowberry (*Symphoricarpos*)

VALUABLE WINTER FLOWERS

Cornus mas
Garrya elliptica
Witch hazel (*Hamamelis*)
Mahonia aqifolium, M. × intermedia
Christmas box (*Sarcococca*)

PLANTING PLANS FOR SHADE

SHADY BORDERS

WHEN PLANNING any planting scheme, the gardener's aim is to produce as long a season of interest as possible. In sun, this may be achieved simply by choosing long-flowering plants, whereas in shade, prolonged interest usually relies more on variations in foliage form, colour and texture. Imaginative arrangements of foliage can be pleasing in their own right, and also provide a long-lasting backdrop to set off seasonal blooms.

USING GOLDEN FOLIAGE

The use of golden-leaved plants is a clever way of introducing colour variation in a shady border, adding brightness and warmth to a palette that might otherwise consist mainly of greens in various hues and tints. Many golden-leaved plants have a tendency to scorch when grown in full light, and so are displayed to their best advantage if protected with some shade, especially during the hottest hours of the day. Plants with white, cream or golden variegation on their leaves also have the positively beneficial effect of lending an impression of light, which helps to brighten dark or gloomy corners in a border. Bear in mind, however, that a few variegated plants, notably the ivies, often need higher light levels than their more shade-tolerant, green-leaved forms to develop their patterns of variegation fully.

LIGHT RELIEF
Hot mid-day sun frequently scorches the foliage of golden-leaved plants, and many need at least part-day shade to produce their best effects.

◄ BRIGHT BORDER *Narrow, shaded beds alongside buildings need not be dull.*

PLAN FOR A SHADY BORDER

This shady border in mid-summer shows the beautiful effects that can be achieved with a very limited colour palette – mostly greens and golds, with seasonal splashes of blue (*Brunnera macrophylla* 'Dawson's White') and rich yellow (*Meconopsis cambrica*). Sculptural plants, like angelica, hostas and euphorbia, provide height and a seasonal series of focal points, with lower layers of alchemilla and ajuga covering the ground at their feet.

PLANTING PLAN

1 3 × *Hosta* 'Birchwood Parky's Gold', 75cm apart
2 5 × *Meconopsis cambrica* ♀, 25cm apart
3 3 × *Alchemilla mollis*, 75cm apart
4 5 × *Lunaria annua* 'Variegata', 30cm apart
5 1 × *Euphorbia characias* subsp. *wulfenii*, spread 1.2m
6 3 × *Ajuga reptans* 'Variegata' ♀, 50cm apart
7 1 × *Hedera helix* 'Buttercup', 2m high on wall
8 3 × *Hakonechloa macra* 'Aureola', 40cm apart
9 3 × *Brunnera macrophylla* 'Dawson's White', 60cm apart
10 1 × *Angelica archangelica*, spread 1.2m
11 3 × *Hosta* 'Gold Standard', 75cm apart

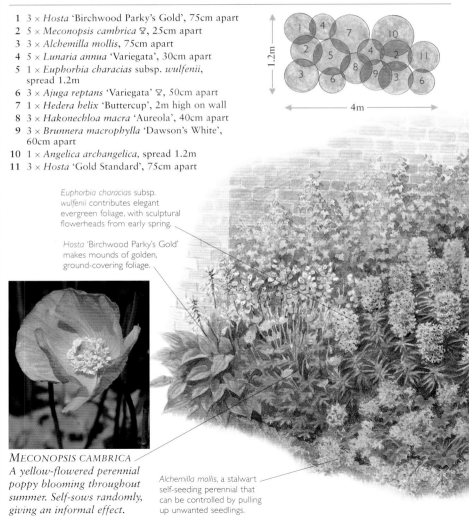

Euphorbia characias subsp. *wulfenii* contributes elegant evergreen foliage, with sculptural flowerheads from early spring.

Hosta 'Birchwood Parky's Gold' makes mounds of golden, ground-covering foliage.

MECONOPSIS CAMBRICA
A yellow-flowered perennial poppy blooming throughout summer. Self-sows randomly, giving an informal effect.

Alchemilla mollis, a stalwart self-seeding perennial that can be controlled by pulling up unwanted seedlings.

ANGELICA ARCHANGELICA is a statuesque biennial with large clusters of yellow-green flowers in summer. It may self-sow, or you can collect its seed when ripe.

MORE CHOICES

SCULPTURAL PLANTS
Aesculus parviflora
Angelica gigas
Aralia elata ♀
× Fatshedera lizei ♀
Kirengeshoma palmata
Matteuccia struthiopteris
Rheum palmatum ♀
Rodgersia pinnata
Sambucus nigra 'Laciniata' ♀,
 S. racemosa 'Plumosa Aurea'

GROUND COVER
Alchemilla alpina
Pachyphragma macrophyllum
Pachysandra terminalis ♀
Pulmonaria many
Sanguinaria canadensis
 'Plena'
Saxifraga × urbium
Tellima grandiflora
Tiarella cordifolia ♀
Waldsteinia ternata

Hedera helix 'Buttercup' is a moderately vigorous ivy ideal for shady walls, with light green leaves that brighten to yellow where sunlight falls on them.

Lunaria annua 'Variegata' is a self-seeding annual or biennial honesty, with red-purple flowers in spring followed by flat, silvery seedpods.

Hosta 'Gold Standard' has heart-shaped leaves in shades of cream, yellow and green.

Ajuga reptans 'Variegata' forms dense, year-round ground cover with blue flower spikes.

Hakonechloa macra 'Aureola' forms an elegant tuft of golden leaves.

Brunnera macrophylla 'Dawson's White' provides foliage interest after its tiny blue flowers fade in early summer.

SHADY TOWN GARDENS

AN ENCLOSED TOWN GARDEN should never be regarded as a damp, dank space with which nothing can be done. Look on it instead as an opportunity to create a cool haven from the noise, heat and dust of the city. Many urban gardens have a strong geometric outline that provides the perfect setting for the elegant formality of a courtyard garden, softened by lush foliage, illuminated by summer flowers and permeated with rich, heady and sensual scents.

A COURTYARD GARDEN

An attractive paved area with plants grown in containers is an ideal solution for city gardens where soil may be altogether absent or of poor quality, and the shelter and warmth of an enclosed, urban space will almost certainly increase the range of plants that you can grow. Containers can be filled with specific compost to suit the individual requirements of each plant. The range of containers is extensive and choosing them for their sculptural qualities will make them a feature in their own right. All but the very largest tubs can be moved around, either to make the most of available light or to provide an ever-changing series of focal points.

PRACTICAL TIPS

• Make the most of available light by painting surrounding walls with reflective, white or pale-coloured masonry paints.
• Choose light-coloured paving slabs or gravel for paths and paved areas, and use pale gravels for top-dressing soil – this also helps to keep down weeds.
• Consider installing a mirror to reflect light and create an illusion of greater space.
• Always remember that whatever the material, plastic, metal or terracotta, all pots must have adequate drainage holes if the plants in them are to thrive.
• When planting up containers, use loam-based composts for weight, stability and superior, long-term nutrient status.

FORMAL PASSAGE
A narrow alleyway has been transformed by the introduction of elegant box topiary, set off against white-painted walls that maximize reflection of ambient light.

◀PERFUMED GARDEN *An enclosed space captures all the fragrance of lilies and tobacco plants.*

PLAN FOR A SHADY COURTYARD

Seen in mid- to late summer, this plan shows the potential of walls and fences for using climbing plants that enjoy shade; sun-loving plants would simply clamber to the top and flower there chiefly for your neighbours' benefit. The depth of shade in an enclosed garden varies with aspect, but the highest levels of light fall in the central area that is fully open to the sky. This part of a garden provides an ideal site for those usually sun-loving plants that often tolerate or thrive in bright shade. A mirror on the far wall amplifies the light and gives the illusion of a formal vista.

ROSA 'ALBERIC BARBIER' is a shade-tolerant, semi-evergreen rambling rose bearing faintly scented white flowers in summer.

Nicotiana alata 'Lime Green', an annual with unusually coloured summer blooms that appear to glow in shade.

Clematis 'Alba Luxurians' has grey-green foliage and small, bell-shaped white flowers from summer to autumn.

MORE CHOICES

FRAGRANT PLANTS

Choisya ternata ♀
Convallaria majalis ♀
Cyclamen hederifolium ♀
Nicotiana sylvestris ♀
Lonicera periclymenum
Rhododendron molle subsp.
  japonicum, R. luteum ♀
Sarcococca most
Viburnum many
Viola odorata

FOR CONTAINERS

Aucuba japonica
  'Crotonifolia' ♀
Begonia grandis
Fargesia nitida ♀
Hydrangea serrata
  'Bluebird' ♀
Osmanthus x *burkwoodii* ♀
Pieris japonica 'Little
  Heath' ♀
Prunus lusitanica ♀
Viburnum carlesii

PLANTING PLAN

1 1 × *Clematis* 'Alba Luxurians' ✿, spread 1.5m
2 1 × *Rosa* 'Albéric Barbier', spread 3m
3 7 × *Nicotiana alata* 'Lime Green' ✿, 25cm apart
4 3 × *Anemone* × *hybrida* 'Honorine Jobert' ✿, 75cm apart
5 1 × *Hosta* 'Frances Williams' ✿, spread 1m
6 1 × *Buxus sempervirens* 'Suffruticosa' ✿, in container; also used as low hedging
7 4 × *Hydrangea quercifolia* ✿, in containers
8 1 × *Rosa* 'New Dawn' ✿, spread 2.5m
9 1 × *Clematis rehderiana* ✿, spread 3m

Hydrangea quercifolia bears cone-shaped white flowerheads in summer, followed by attractive autumn tints.

'New Dawn' is a healthy, vigorous rose bearing several flushes of fragrant pink flowers during summer.

ANEMONE × *HYBRIDA* '*HONORINE JOBERT*' *has cup-shaped glowing white flowers amid clumps of pretty foliage, borne in long succession from mid-summer onwards.*

Buxus sempervirens 'Suffruticosa' is the perfect dwarf box for border edging or topiary.

Clematis rehderiana produces tubular, bell-shaped yellow flowers with a distinct cowslip scent, in mid-summer and autumn.

Hosta 'Frances Williams' forms substantial mounds of thick-textured, puckered, blue-green leaves with yellow variegation, and scented summer flowers.

PLANTING UNDER TREES

F EW GARDENS ARE LARGE ENOUGH to accommodate a woodland garden, but
many have one or two trees. Planting beneath them can often prove difficult,
because venturing roots take moisture and nutrients from the soil. Some trees,
though, have deep tap roots, rather than surface roots. If you are fortunate in
having such trees, or choose new trees carefully (*see overleaf*), underplanting can
be more exciting – and certainly more successful than grassing the area.

LETTING IN MORE LIGHT

Sometimes, it is desirable to increase
the light levels beneath trees, especially
where you intend to introduce extensive
underplanting. Letting in more light
is best done by lifting or thinning the
canopy (*see below*).

If trees and their lower branches are
small enough for this to be carried out
by hand with a bow saw, you can safely
tackle the task yourself. With mature trees
and heavy, dense branchwork, however,
removing large branches is an extremely
dangerous job that should be left to
a professional arboriculturist.

TREE SURGERY

Poor or careless tree surgery can be
expensive to rectify and may even result
in a tree being lost altogether. When
looking for an arboriculturist, or tree
surgeon, therefore, opt for a recommended
professional and ask for a site visit and
assessment before any work is carried
out. Obtain assurance that all felled
wood will be removed from the site if
you so wish, and that any liability for
damage or compensation claims is their,
not your, responsibility.

Height of
the clear trunk
is increased

CROWN LIFTING
*Crown lifting is when the lower branches
of a tree are removed to allow easy access
beneath or to admit more light.*

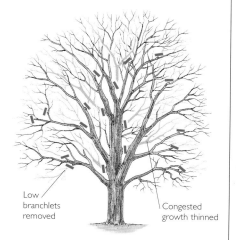

Low
branchlets
removed

Congested
growth thinned

CROWN THINNING
*Crown thinning involves the removal of up to
one-third of the growth on main branches,
to allow more light through the tree's canopy.*

◄ A RAISED CANOPY *Tall-trunked trees allow spring flowers to make a colourful underplanting.* •

CREATING A SHADY HOLLOW

A tree is often among the first additions to be considered in a new garden, and with careful choice, you can greatly increase the scope for attractive underplanting. Deep-rooting deciduous trees with slender, bare trunks and light, airy canopies allow the plants below to thrive without too much competition from tree roots. A flowering tree with plants in flower below (as here, in early summer) creates a superb focal point.

STYRAX JAPONICUS
A deep-rooting small tree of light airy habit, with summer flowers and good autumn colour. Good for small gardens and underplanting.

Iris sibirica 'Lady of Quality' forms attractive clumps of narrow, fresh green leaves and glowing blue-violet flowers in early summer.

Bergenia purpurascens has purple-red flowers in spring. The leathery dark green leaves turn red-purple in winter.

Polygonatum x hybridum has elegant foliage and bell-shaped white flowers borne on arching stems.

Actaea alba bears white flowers in spring and summer, followed by clusters of white berries in autumn.

Primula florindae is a rosette-forming perennial with fragrant, pale yellow flowers in summer.

PLANTING PLAN

1 3 × *Iris sibirica* 'Lady of Quality', 60cm apart
2 3 × *Bergenia purpurascens* ✷, 30cm apart
3 1 × *Styrax japonicus*, spread to 8m
4 3 × *Polygonatum* × *hybridum* ✷, 30cm apart
5 3 × *Primula florindae* ✷, 75cm apart
6 3 × *Actaea alba* ✷, 60cm apart
7 3 × *Aconitum* 'Ivorine', 45cm apart
8 3 × *Campanula persicifolia* 'Telham Beauty', 75cm apart
9 3 × *Dicentra spectabilis* 'Alba' ✷, 40cm apart
10 3 × *Anemone sylvestris*, 50cm apart
11 1 × *Polystichum setiferum* Divisilobum Group, spread 50–70cm

2.5m

3m

CAMPANULA
PERSICIFOLIA
'TELHAM BEAUTY'
*bears luminous blue
flowers over long
periods from early
summer, especially if
regularly deadheaded.*

Dicentra spectabilis 'Alba'
flowers from early summer
for longer periods than the
pink-flowered species.

Polystichum setiferum
Divisilobum Group has
finely divided, fresh green
fronds that provide
textural interest
throughout the year.

CHOOSING TREES

**Good choices for under-
planting in small gardens**
Acer capillipes ✷,
  A. davidii
Betula albosinensis
Carya cordiformis ✷
Celtis occidentalis
Cercis canadensis, especially
  'Forest Pansy' ✷
*Cornus controversa, C.
  'Eddie's White Wonder'* ✷,
  *C. florida, C. mas,
  C. nuttallii*
Sophora japonica ✷
Sorbus most species
Styrax obassia
Zelkova serrata ✷

Aconitum 'Ivorine' has
divided, fresh green foliage
and spires of creamy
flowers in early summer.

Anemone sylvestris is a
spreading perennial with
delicate white flowers in late
spring and early summer.

PLANTING UNDER A LARGE TREE

A large, mature tree in leaf will shade a wide area of ground by mid-summer; use shrubs to give height and structure to planting below, interplanted with perennials that will really thrive in the double shade of the tree canopy and the larger plants. The dappled shade cast by this stately oak (*Quercus robur*) is accentuated by the choice of mainly white-flowered plants growing underneath, shown here as summer turns to autumn.

PLANTING PLAN

1 3 × *Tricyrtis hirta*, 60cm apart
2 1 × *Hydrangea paniculata* 'Grandiflora' ♀, spread 2.5m
3 3 × *Actaea rubra* ♀, 30cm apart
4 1 × *Quercus robur* ♀, spread to 25m
5 3 × *Gentiana asclepiadea* ♀, 45cm apart
6 3 × *Phegopteris connectilis*, 50cm apart
7 3 × *Vancouveria hexandra*, 40cm apart
8 3 × *Nicotiana sylvestris* ♀, 60cm apart
9 3 × *Lilium martagon*, 30cm apart
10 1 × *Fothergilla major* ♀, spread 2m
11 3 × *Hakonechloa macra* 'Aureola' ♀, 40cm apart

2.5m

4m

Gentiana asclepiadea is a clump-forming perennial with rich blue or white, bell-shaped flowers in late summer and autumn.

HYDRANGEA PANICULATA 'GRANDIFLORA' *is a deciduous shrub with large, white flowerheads borne from late summer and good colour in autumn.*

Tricyrtis hirta spreads by rhizomes. An unusual perennial, it bears funnel-shaped, white flowers with purple spots in autumn.

NICOTIANA SYLVESTRIS is a robust woodland biennial bearing dense panicles of very fragrant white flowers throughout summer.

MORE CHOICES

GOOD-VALUE SHRUBS
Amelanchier canadensis,
  A. laevis, A. lamarckii ♥
Callicarpa bodinieri,
  C. bodinieri var. giraldii
Cornus mas ♥
Enkianthus most
Mahonia aquifolium
Pyracantha most
Rhododendrons
Viburnum x burkwoodii

GROUND COVER
Alchemilla alpina,
  A. conjuncta
Arctostaphylos uva-ursi
Blechnum penna-marina
Brunnera macrophylla ♥
Euphorbia amygdaloides
  var. robbiae
Gaultheria mucronata ♥
Geranium macrorrhizum
Maianthemum bifolium

Quercus robur is a large, deep-rooting deciduous tree that casts ideal dappled shade for plants below.

Lilium martagon, a bulbous perennial with pink to purple-red turkscap flowers in mid-summer.

Actaea rubra has spires of white flowers in early summer, followed by glossy red berries in autumn.

Fothergilla major is a deciduous shrub with stunning autumn colour and scented, white bottle-brush flowers in spring.

Hakonechloa macra 'Aureola', is a clump-forming woodland grass with good autumn colour.

Phegopteris connectilis spreads by rhizomes. The delicate, fresh green fronds of this fern make good ground cover throughout the season.

Vancouveria hexandra is a creeping ground-cover perennial with lobed, bright green leaves and tiny white flowers in early summer.

DAMP SHADE

MANY GARDENS POSSESS A DAMP, shady corner, often inherited from previous owners and frequently uninspiring, but with thoughtful planting they can become an admirable feature in their own right. Although they are often in permanent shade, this may be graduated from light to deep, or dappled, and the cool and humid conditions will suit a wide range of shade- and moisture-loving plants. In most cases, the only major improvement needed is the incorporation of organic matter before planting and an annual mulch or feed. For decorative interest and atmosphere, add a small, bubbling or trickling water feature.

PROBLEM-SOLVING PLANTS

To avoid having to do too much work in damp shady areas and compacting the soil, consider a scheme that is based on low-maintenance ground-cover plants. Ivies and deadnettles (*Lamium*) make superb cover for "problem" sites, tolerating both damp and dry shade and poor soil. Ivies, together with climbing hydrangeas, are also the ideal choice for permanently shaded walls and fences. Most ground-cover plants spread quickly by means of creeping roots or rooting stems. You can mulch between plants while they are small (*see p.48*) to suppress weed growth between them until they grow and mingle together.

Good preparation is crucial for successful ground cover. If it is not done properly, it becomes a tangled mat that is hopelessly intertwined with weeds, which are extremely difficult to eradicate without damage to ornamental plants. The most important part of preparation, therefore, is to clear the ground thoroughly of all weeds, especially perennial ones like couch grass. Spraying with a systemic weedkiller is the quickest method. If you don't wish to use chemicals, weeds can be removed by hand when digging over or, if you are planning well ahead, covered and suppressed with black plastic or old carpet.

LIGHTENING THE WORKLOAD
This low-maintenance scheme uses closely planted ground cover as a horizontal foil for the vertical element provided by ivy scrambling over an old tree trunk. Bare soil is mulched to suppress weeds.

◄ MOISTURE LOVERS *Arum lilies provide focal points in a streamside setting in shade.*

PLAN FOR DAMP SHADE

In this design for a damp shady spot, shade is cast by high adjacent walls and by the airy-leaved birch tree, although lightened by the birch's bright white trunk. The back wall is clothed with climbing hydrangea, which provides a strong vertical element to the design of the scheme and an interesting winter framework. A carpet of ground cover is used as a foil for a succession of flowers that change with the seasons.

DIGITALIS PURPUREA 'ALBA'
A biennial with spires of creamy-white flowers, whose season can be prolonged with autumn and spring sowings.

Brunnera macrophylla offers sprays of small, pure blue flowers in spring, and then beautifully textured leaves that enlarge after flowering.

Betula ermanii 'Grayswood Hill' is an elegant, airy tree with glowing, pure white bark. It casts light, dappled shade.

Helleborus niger 'Potter's Wheel' has bowl-shaped, green-eyed white flowers from early winter. Remove last year's leaves to display flowers to best effect.

HEDERA HELIX 'GLACIER'
forms a ground-covering carpet of grey-green leaves marbled with silver-grey. Plant at the margins of the shade-casting canopy.

Helleborus x *hybridus* 'Ballard's Black' makes a dramatic contrast plant with its deep, dark purple flowers borne in late winter and spring.

PLANTING PLAN

1   3 × *Digitalis purpurea* f. *albiflora*,
    60cm apart

2   3 × *Brunnera macrophylla* ♥,
    60cm apart

3   3 × *Helleborus niger* 'Potter's Wheel',
    45cm apart

4   1 × *Betula ermanii* 'Grayswood Hill' ♥,
    spread to 12m

5   3 × *Helleborus* × *hybridus* 'Ballard's Black',
    45cm apart

6   3 × *Hedera helix* 'Glacier' ♥, 1m apart

7   3 × *Astilbe* 'Irrlicht', 50cm apart

8   8 × *Astrantia* 'Shaggy' ♥, 45cm apart

9   3 × *Pulmonaria officinalis* 'Sissinghurst
    White' ♥, 45cm apart

10 1 × *Hydrangea anomala* subsp.
    petiolaris ♥, spread to 15m

11 3 × *Epimedium grandiflorum* 'Rose
    Queen' ♥, 30cm apart

12 5 × *Lamium maculatum* 'Beacon Silver' ♥,
    75cm apart

2m

2.5m

Hydrangea petiolaris produces creamy flowers in summer, set off against dark leaves that turn yellow in autumn.

Astilbe 'Irrlicht' has creamy-white plumes above finely divided, dark green leaves in spring and early summer. They persist into winter.

SELF-SEEDERS

Flowering plants that may pop up randomly among ground cover include:

Aquilegia vulgaris
Arum italicum
  'Marmoratum' ♥
Chelidonium majus
Chionodoxa forbesii
Digitalis purpurea
Geranium phaeum
Honesty *(Lunaria annua)*
Meconopsis cambrica
Ornithogalum
  montanum
Polemonium pauciflorum
Scilla siberica ♥
Viola odorata

Epimedium grandiflorum 'Rose Queen' produces deep bronze-purple new leaves and spurred, rose-pink flowers in spring.

Pulmonaria officinalis 'Sissinghurst White' bears white flowers in late spring, above silvery, white-spangled leaves that come into their full beauty after flowering.

Lamium maculatum 'Beacon Silver': good ground cover with clear pink, summer flowers and silver leaves. Tolerates poor, dry soils too.

Special Plant Collections

M AKE A FEATURE OF A COOL, shady spot by using it to display one of the beautiful foliage plant groups that need these conditions. Working with a restricted colour palette, as with ferns, or with similar leaf shapes, as with hostas, makes it all the more fascinating – even addictive – to design schemes that associate and contrast different textures and hues. Specimens of different heights will give structure and variety to your composition.

Making a Feature of Ferns

As a group, ferns can be fairly considered as the ultimate shade plants and could hardly be better designed for use in places where light levels are low. They tend to have been rather neglected since the early part of this century, but are now, once again, being appreciated for their beauty and versatility.

In Victorian England, displays of plant collections were large and theatrical, and ferneries would be embellished by props such as moss-covered "fallen" trees, grottoes and cascades. Such a feature is not difficult to scale down for a small garden, and fun to design and build – or, you may prefer to integrate your fern collection more into the garden by introducing a few other, complementary plants among them. Use other foliage plants with sculptural qualities to create

FERN-GROWING TIPS

• A cool, humid, shady site, with a moisture-retentive, humus-rich soil and some shelter from strong, cold or drying winds is all that most ferns ask. Work as much organic matter into your soil before planting as you can.
• Provide filtering shelter from wind with barrier plantings or hedges. Solid barriers can create harmful turbulence in their lee.

strong textural contrasts. Rodgersias, hostas, rheums and grasses suit this purpose well, and for lower-level planting, use neat-leaved ground cover like *Vancouveria* and *Waldsteinia*. Introduce flower colour with woodlanders like dicentras, *Chelidonium majus* or *Meconopsis cambrica*, which self-sow to produce beautiful natural effects.

TAKING COVER
In this courtyard garden, planting in paving crevices provides ideal cool, damp conditions at the plants' roots. Ferns that spread by rhizomes, like Phegopteris *and* Gymnocarpium, *are eager to infiltrate paving crevices.*

◀ DISTINCTIVE FRONDS *Ferns are seen at their best when back-lit by dappled sunlight.*

PLAN FOR A SMALL FERNERY

This design exploits ferns' natural diversity of form. Tall shuttlecocks of finely divided fronds, like those of *Matteuccia*, are used in contrast with creeping, rhizomatous ferns, such as *Phegopteris*, which spread to form a verdant carpet. The colour range includes many shades of green, enhanced by the spring tints of emerging croziers, a golden grass and gold-splashed hosta, and the yellow of Welsh poppies (*Meconopsis cambrica*).

PLANTING PLAN

1 3 × *Meconopsis cambrica*, 25cm apart
2 1 × *Phegopteris connectilis*, spread to 50cm
3 1 × *Adiantum venustum*, spread to 50cm
4 1 × *Matteuccia struthiopteris*, spread to 1m
5 1 × *Athyrium niponicum* 'Pictum', spread to 50cm
6 3 × *Carex elata* 'Aurea', 45cm apart
7 1 × *Asplenium scolopendrium* 'Crispum', spread to 60cm
8 3 × *Osmunda cinnamomea*, 60cm apart
9 1 × *Polypodium vulgare* 'Cornubiense', spread to 60cm
10 1 × *Hosta fortunei* 'Albomarginata', spread to 80cm
11 1 × *Polystichum setiferum* Divisilobum Group, spread to 60cm

Matteuccia struthiopteris, a shuttlecock fern with arching, finely divided, pale green sterile fronds and, from mid-summer, central clumps of dark brown fertile fronds.

Meconopsis cambrica is a self-seeding perennial with bluish-green leaves and orange or golden yellow flowers borne throughout summer.

Phegopteris connectilis is a carpet-forming fern with soft triangular fronds of pale bright green.

Adiantum venustum is a creeping fern. The fan-shaped, bright green segments are held on glossy black stalks and are bright bronze-pink as they unfurl in spring.

Athyrium niponicum 'Pictum' has finely divided fronds that are unusual in being variegated. The silver-grey frond segments complement red-purple stalks.

MORE PLANTS TO GROW WTH FERNS

Alchemilla mollis	*Dicentra spectabilis*
Arum italicum 'Marmoratum'	*Galium odoratum*
Asarum europaeum	Hellebores
Bergenias	*Kirengeshoma palmata*
Cornus canadensis	*Podophyllum hexandrum*
Corydalis lutea	*Tellima grandiflora*

POLYPODIUM VULGARE 'CORNUBIENSE' *is a vigorous, ground-covering fern with variably divided fronds of interesting texture.*

Osmunda cinnamomea is a deciduous shuttlecock fern, with pale blue-green sterile fronds and upright, central fertile fronds bearing cinnamon-brown spores, which persist into winter.

POLYSTICHUM SETIFERUM DIVISILOBUM GROUP *has shuttlecocks of soft-textured fronds divided finely into very narrow segments.*

Carex elata 'Aurea', a creeping golden sedge, forms clumps of narrow, arching leaves of rich yellow margined with green.

Asplenium scolopendrium 'Crispum' is an evergreen fern producing shuttlecocks of strap-shaped, glossy, bright green fronds with wavy margins.

Hosta fortunei 'Albomarginata' forms substantial mounds of large, heart-shaped, deeply veined leaves of olive-green with irregular golden margins.

CARING FOR PLANTS IN SHADE

PREPARING AND PLANTING

T HE MOST IMPORTANT first step is to assess the type of shade in your
site, then to choose only those plants that will really be suited by your
conditions. But there is also plenty of practical help to give plants right
at the start that will ensure satisfying results, and less work in the future.

IMPROVING GROWING CONDITIONS

Before you buy any plants, prepare the soil
well (*see overleaf*), clearing weeds and
improving the soil structure. Consider
whether there is anything else you can do
to make the site more conducive to plant
growth – painting a wall white to reflect in
more light, for example, or thinning

existing shrubs (*see below*) so that they cast
less shade on the ground. Thinning also
benefits shrubs that grow in shade, letting
in light and air around their branches and
on to plants below. Check in a reference
guide to discover the specific pruning needs
of your shrubs before making cuts.

THINNING FROM THE BASE
*Shrubs that form a thicket of
upright or arching stems can
be thinned by cutting out
some main stems right at the
base. Remove one in three or
four in any one year, choosing
the oldest. You may need
loppers or a pruning saw; do
not overstrain and damage
secateurs on thick stems.*

COPPICING

Shrubs that can be cut hard
back in early spring every
year or two include hazel,
smoke bush (*Cotinus*), elder
(*Sambucus*), and some dog-
woods (*Cornus*) and willows.
The extra light, especially in
spring, will increase your
choice of underplanting.

THINNING BUSHY GROWTH
*Thin shrubs with branching
stems not by trimming back
side-branches, but by cutting
main stems down to a new,
upright sideshoot. Don't
worry if it looks awkward at
first: the growth on this shoot
as it becomes the new
"branch leader" will soon
make it arch over attractively.*

◀ EYE-CATCHERS *Good preparation and care help ensure that you get the very best from plants.*

PREPARING THE SITE

Pre-planting preparations benefit the future health of your soil and plants. Dig over new planting areas in the season before you intend to plant, to give the soil time to settle. This also allows time before planting to use a systemic weedkiller on any perennial weeds – or, remove by hand as you dig. Incorporate plenty of well-rotted organic matter (humus); it improves the drainage and workability of clay soils and increases the nutrient content and moisture-retentiveness of light soils.

IMPROVING THE SOIL
On new ground, work in organic matter (see below) *to a spade's depth when digging over. This is hard work but worthwhile, and seldom needs to be repeated. It is usually sufficient to fork in organic matter into the top 8–10cm of areas to be planted under trees and in established borders, avoiding damage to existing plants' roots.*

MAKE A MULCH

The leaf fall from deciduous garden trees is a ready source of leaf mould. Make your own organic soil additive or mulch by raking them up and stacking in a circular bin made from chicken wire around stakes, about 1m tall and wide. If shredded first, the leaves will decompose quickly and be ready to use by the following spring.

MANURE
Well-rotted manure adds some nutrients and plentiful humus.

MUSHROOM COMPOST
Rich in humus but contains lime.

GARDEN COMPOST
Fine soil improver, containing humus and valuable nutrients.

LEAF MOULD
Low-level nutrients and humus; makes a natural-looking mulch.

PROVIDING ACCESS

Soil structure is easily compacted when wet, leading to a shortage of oxygen at the plant roots and poor drainage. Most shade-lovers need moist soils, which makes it difficult to gain access for dead-heading and other routine tasks without treading on the site. To avoid damaging soil and plants, add a platform or some stepping stones from which you can work, using natural materials such as log sections, or by laying small pavers within a border; these will quickly be disguised by plant growth.

PLANTING POT-GROWN PLANTS

Plants grown in containers can be planted at any time that the soil is not frozen or baked dry, but they must be watered regularly until well-established. They should be planted at the same level as in their pots, but this can make them difficult to water properly because of runoff. If the water permeates only the surface layers, roots tend to grow up towards the surface to reach it, where they will be even more exposed to heat and drought. You can mound up a ring of soil around the plant to make a dip that will hold water, or add a watering pipe (*right*). Drip-feed systems or seep-hoses are especially convenient for groups of plants, supplying water directly to the soil surface above the root zone of each one; they are best used with a timer to avoid unnecessary waste.

Water applied through angled pipe

Balanced root growth

REACHING THE ROOTS
Position a section of old plastic pipe at an angle to the plant, so that one end is near to the root zone and the other end is open to the air at or just within the plant's canopy. Water can then be applied directly to the roots.

SPECIAL PLANTING NEEDS

Buy spring-flowering bulbs in autumn, and vice versa. Most should be planted at a depth 2–3 times their height, setting larger bulbs deeper. Tie climbers, even self-clinging ones, into supports to help them grow away. Trees, shrubs and climbers may be sold bare-rooted, or with their roots wrapped or bagged with a little compost. Buy and plant these only in autumn or spring. Autumn plantings should establish well in cool, rainy weather, but spring may be safer in cold areas. Dig a hole twice the width of the rootball and 1½ times its depth. Spread out the roots in the hole and adjust the depth so that the soil level will match the soil mark on the stem or stems. Backfill and firm in, then water and mulch (*see p.50*). Water regularly until established.

PLANTING CLIMBERS
To give a young climber more light before training it into a host shrub, train it first up a pole next to the shrub so it can grow up and over the host's branches, rather than struggling through them.

PLANTING SNOWDROPS
Snowdrops are not planted as dry bulbs, but "in the green", looking rather like spring onions. Firm them in gently and keep well-watered, and the foliage should soon perk up.

ROUTINE PLANT CARE

KEEP THE SITE WEED-FREE and check regularly for any problems (*see overleaf*). Most plants need little or no additional fertilizer in woodland soils, as the annual leaf fall recycles plant nutrients. Elsewhere, apply a high-potash feed (such as tomato feed) or balanced slow-release fertilizer in early spring to improve growth and flower production. Regular deadheading helps to encourage more blooms.

FEEDING AND MULCHING

Always apply feeds at the manufacturers' recommended rate, as plant roots can be damaged by applications that are too heavy. Shield any top growth from contact with the feed as it will burn the leaves.

Fork fertilizer in lightly, taking care not to damage shallow roots, then apply an annual mulch. Ornamental foliage plants, like hostas, benefit from an additional liquid feed during the growing season.

WOODCHIPS

GRAVEL

HOW TO APPLY FERTILIZER
Sprinkle directly on to damp soil a little way from the plant base. Fork in lightly to avoid roots.

MULCHING GROUND-COVER
A 5–10cm layer of shredded bark, woodchips, leaf mould or gravel between plants keeps moisture in.

PLANTING THROUGH SHEET MULCHES

Sheet mulches allow complete weed control beneath plants that grow from a single stem, and help to conserve moisture and regulate soil temperature. Fibre fleeces or landscaping fabric are permeable to air and water and allow fertilizer to be applied when required. Remove any perennial weeds before mulching, and lay it onto damp soil. Remember to perforate black plastic sheeting to allow the passage of water. To plant through a sheet mulch, make a cross-shaped incision in the sheet just large enough to insert a plant. Fold back the sheet corners when planting, and water well before adding a top-dressing.

FINISHING TOUCH
Top-dress sheet mulches with natural-looking materials such as cocoa shells, bark chips or gravel, for an attractive finish.

KEEPING UP APPEARANCES

In autumn, tidy up herbaceous plants that are dying back, not for neatness, but for good garden hygiene; many plants will succumb to rots if overwintered with wet, decomposing material at their crowns. Cut down flowered stems and trim top growth from perennials, using secateurs or shears. Pick fallen leaves out of plants by hand, and rake up those on the ground using a spring-tine rake or garden broom. Use them to make leaf mould (see p.48) for mulching. Some evergreen perennials, most notably epimediums and hellebores, benefit from special treatment in spring to give their best (see right). Do not, however, trim back the foliage of spring bulbs after flowering; the plants need to keep it until it dies naturally to build up their strength.

SHOWING OFF SPRING FLOWERS
Cut out old, dark green leaves at the base in late winter or early spring, when the emerging flowerbuds and new foliage shoots are visible.

TRIMMING OVER
Some ground cover plants can be given a "haircut" with a nylon line trimmer to remove tatty foliage. Do this in autumn or very early spring, to avoid damaging any new shoots.

Plants that can be trimmed over: *Euphorbia amygdaloides* var. *robbiae, Hypericum calycinum, H. androsaemum, Vinca major*

SUCKER REMOVAL
Suckers from roots sap a plant's energy. Trace them to their point of origin and pull them off with a sharp tug. Neaten the wound with a sharp knife to remove nearby dormant buds.

Plants prone to producing suckers: Grafted plants, including *Hamamelis* cultivars and roses, *Aralia elata, Amelanchier canadensis*

REMOVING REVERTED SHOOTS
Cut out reverted, or all-green, shoots that appear on variegated plants, as they are more vigorous and may become dominant over variegated growth.

Plants prone to reversion: *Aralia elata* 'Variegata', *Euonymus fortunei* 'Silver Queen', *Aucuba japonica* 'Crotonifolia'

REMOVING NON-VARIEGATED SHOOTS
Remove any plain gold or cream shoots on variegated plants, as they make the plant less able to use limited light resources efficiently when grown in a shady site.

Prone to producing all cream/yellow leaves: All white-leaved plants, *Euonymus fortunei* 'Silver Queen', *E. fortunei* 'Emerald 'n' Gold'

KEEPING PLANTS HEALTHY

REGULAR TOURS OF INSPECTION of your plants, removing weeds while small or simply picking off pests or any diseased stems or leaves, can prevent many problems taking a hold. If problems do become severe, ask at a garden centre for advice if you wish to use a chemical control, and follow the manufacturer's instructions carefully. Where possible, use organic or "natural" methods or pest-specific chemicals, to avoid killing beneficial creatures that attack pests.

FRIENDS AND FOES

Shaded sites, particularly when well planted and mulched, will be cool in summer and cosy in winter, attracting all manner of creatures. Learn to identify between garden friends and foes before reaching for deterrents. Hedgehogs, thrushes, frogs, toads and shrews all eat slugs and insect pests, but are vulnerable to garden chemicals, so if you want to encourage wildlife into the garden, do not eliminate pests too assiduously, to leave beneficial creatures something to feed on. Woodlice tend to damage seedlings under glass, but are welcomed outdoors for their habit of recycling dead plant material. Aphid and caterpillar pests will be less common since they prefer sun, but slugs and snails (*see below*) will congregate in cool, moist sites.

MOSTLY HARMLESS
In open gardens or woodland, woodlice live in the surface layers of soil and are primarily recyclers of organic material. They tend only to harm young seedlings.

GARDEN SNAILS
These unwelcome visitors are active in the cool of the evening, making holes in foliage and leaving behind silver slime trails.

CONTROLLING PESTS

The key enemies to plants in shade are slugs and snails. Active between spring and autumn, they rasp away holes in foliage, leaving trails of silver slime behind them. There are a number of controls, both chemical and "organic": for the ultimate in natural methods, prowl the garden on damp evenings by torchlight, picking off the pests by hand and disposing of them where they can do no harm.

Chemical controls Slug pellets and dusts containing chemical ingredients such as methiocarb control both slugs and snails. Some are now labelled as safe for children and pets, but even so, family gardeners may prefer not to use them.

Biological control The parasite *Phasmarhabditis hermaphrodita* will destroy slugs and snails. Some garden centres stock it, or it is available through mail order. Most suppliers recommend applying it twice, with a two-week interval.

Traps and barriers A mulch of sharp grit or holly clippings sometimes helps to deter these pests. There are several traps that gardeners find effective: a jar of beer sunk into the ground and an upturned empty grapefruit half are the most popular. The trap's contents can be disposed of in the morning.

A CALENDAR OF SEASONAL REMINDERS

SPRING

• As soon as soil is workable, plant and mulch new perennials.

• Clump-forming summer- and autumn-flowering perennials that are overcrowded can be lifted, carefully split into portions with shoots and plenty of roots, and replanted, spaced more widely apart.

• Remove dead leaves from plant crowns.

• Plant or transplant evergreen shrubs.

• Prune established evergreen shrubs, and shrubs that flower after mid-summer.

• Apply fertilizer to established plants, followed by a mulch on to damp, weed-free soil.

• Set in place supports for tall-stemmed perennials, where necessary.

• Divide crowded bulbs after flowering; make a note of bare spots that could be filled with new bulbs in autumn.

SUMMER

• Divide and replant crowded clumps of spring bulbs before foliage fades.

• Make a note of where summer perennials could be planted to hide the dying foliage of spring bulbs.

• Check that creeping, rooting perennials are not overwhelming others. You can dig up rooted portions and use them to plant up bare ground elsewhere.

• Set out young annuals and bedding plants.

• Check for and deal with pests and diseases as seen.

• Clear weeds and replenish mulches as necessary.

• Keep new plantings well-watered until established. Pay special attention to watering plants in containers.

• Prune spring-flowering shrubs after flowering.

• Deadhead perennials and shrubs, if necessary, after flowering.

AUTUMN

• Plant young biennials in their flowering site.

• Clump-forming spring-flowering perennials that are overcrowded can be lifted, carefully split into portions with shoots and plenty of roots, and replanted, more widely apart.

• Plant spring-flowering bulbs.

• Clear autumn leaves and make leaf mould.

• Add disease-free, dead plant material to compost heap.

• Apply dry mulches of bracken litter, hay or conifer branches to plants that need winter protection, especially in areas without snow cover.

• Plant bare-rooted shrubs or trees during mild weather when the soil is workable. Water them in thoroughly until established and mulch well. Withhold fertilizer in the first year after planting to encourage the roots to search more widely for nutrients.

WINTER

• Order catalogues from nurseries to select new plants for your garden.

• Where branches are small enough to be handled safely, remove those that are too low from deciduous trees to let in more light. To remove large branches from mature trees, consult a qualified arborist.

• Shake snow from trees and shrubs to avoid breakage.

• Protect vulnerable plants in containers from hard frosts and evergreens from cold, dry winds. Garden fleece or plastic bubble-wrap can be used as blankets.

• Identify gaps where a winter-flowering shrub would be attractive, and make a note of planting sites for late winter bulbs, like aconites and snowdrops.

• As spring begins, remove dry winter mulches and other cold protection only when threat of hard frosts is over.

DEADHEADING RHODODENDRONS
Remove dead flowers by pinching them out with your finger and thumb to avoid damage to the new buds that form directly under the old one.

USING LEAVES
Gather up fallen leaves and decaying fruits and let them decompose to make leaf mould – a soil improver that is particularly enjoyed by acid-loving woodland plants

PLANTS FOR SHADE

THE RANGE OF SHADE-LOVING plants here have symbols that indicate their preferred conditions, but many are not unduly demanding. Nearly all are completely hardy; a few may need protection from severe cold. More growing tips for plants here may be found in *Caring for Your Plants (see pp.47–53)*.

KEY TO SYMBOLS ◨ *Prefers partial shade* ▨ *Prefers light or dappled shade* ▧ *Tolerates deep shade* ◊ *Prefers well-drained soil* ◗ *Prefers moist soil* ◆ *Prefers wet soil* ᶜ *Needs acid soil* ✻ *Half hardy – can withstand temperatures down to 0°C* ✻✻ *Frost hardy – can withstand temperatures down to –5°C* ✻✻✻ *Fully hardy – can withstand temperatures down to –15°C* **Tall** *More than 1.2m high* **Medium** *60cm to 1.2m high* **Small** *Less than 60cm high* ♀ *RHS Award of Garden Merit*

A

Aconitum (Monkshood)
Medium to tall, herbaceous perennials with lobed leaves and spikes of hooded, blue flowers in mid- to late summer. For informal and mixed or herbaceous borders. All parts are toxic.
◨ ▨ ◊ ✻✻✻
A. 'Ivorine' *p.34.* Also recommended: *A. carmichaelii* 'Arendsii', *A. hemsleyanum*, *A. napellus*.

Actaea (Baneberry)
Small to medium perennials bearing rounded sprays of white flowers in spring and early summer, followed by red or white berries in autumn. For informal plantings or woodland gardens.
◨ ▨ ▧ ◊ ✻✻✻
A. alba ♀ *p.34; A. rubra* ♀ *p.36.*

Adiantum venustum
(Himalayan maidenhair fern)
Small, evergreen, spreading fern valued for its black stalks and distinctive, mid-green triangular fronds. New fronds are bright bronze-pink when they emerge in late winter and early spring.
◨ ▨ ◊ ✻✻✻
A. venustum ♀ *p.44.*

ADIANTUM VENUSTUM

Aesculus parviflora ♀
(Buckeye)
Tall, wide-spreading shrub bearing white flowers in mid-summer. Noted for its tolerance of a range of soils and sites. For woodland gardens or shrub borders.
◨ ▨ ◊ ◗ ✻✻✻

Ajuga (Bugle)
Small, spreading perennials valued for their spikes of deep blue flowers and mats of glossy, often coloured, foliage. For woodland and borders.
◨ ▨ ▧ ◊ ◗ ✻✻✻
A. pyramidalis p.40;
A. reptans 'Variegata' *p.26.*

Akebia quinata
(Chocolate vine)
Tall, twining climber bearing purple-brown flowers in spring, followed by purple fruits. For walls, arbours, or through trees.
◨ ▨ ◊ ✻✻✻

◀ SHADY CORNER *Tall, distinctive ferns and variegated foliage create an atmospheric setting.*

Alchemilla (Lady's mantle)
Small, ground-covering,
herbaceous perennials with
silky-haired leaves and sprays
of yellow-green flowers borne
in summer. Self-sows freely.
◨ ◪ ❋ ◊ ◊ ✳✳✳
A. mollis ♀ *p.26*. Also
recommended: *A. alpina*,
A. conjuncta.

Amelanchier lamarckii ♀
(Juneberry)
Tall, suckering shrub bearing
sprays of white flowers in
spring and early summer,
followed by purple-black
fruits. Noted for its bronze
foliage in autumn. For
shrub borders or woodland.
◨ ◪ ◊ ◊ ❦ ✳✳✳

Anemone (Windflower)
Tall, autumn-flowering
herbaceous or small, spring-
flowering tuberous perennials
bearing cup-shaped flowers
in white, blue, pink or red.
Thrive in borders and
woodland gardens beneath
deciduous shrubs or trees.
◨ ◪ ◊ ◊ ✳✳✳
A. × hybrida 'Honorine
Jobert' ♀ *p.30*; *A. sylvestris*
p.34.

Angelica
Tall, herbaceous plants with
sprays of small, greenish
flowers, followed by ribbed,
brown fruits. Use as focal
points in borders. May self-
sow. Need deep, fertile soil.
◨ ◪ ❋ ◊ ✳✳✳
A. archangelica p.26.

Aquilegia vulgaris
(Columbine)
Medium-height herbaceous
perennial valued for its
rosettes of leaves and sprays
of spurred, bell-shaped
flowers, in shades of white,
pink, red or blue, borne in
late spring and early summer.
For cottage gardens and
herbaceous or mixed borders.
◨ ◪ ◊ ✳✳✳
Recommended: 'Norah
Barlow' ♀.

Arctostaphylos uva-ursi
(Bearberry)
Small, evergreen, ground-
covering shrub with tangled
branches bearing small, oval
leaves. Tiny, pink-rimmed
flowers are borne in summer,
followed by red autumn
fruits. For woodland gardens.
◨ ◪ ◊ ❦ ✳✳✳

Arum (Lords-and-ladies)
Small, low-growing perennials
with spear-shaped leaves,
marked silvery-white, and
hooded spikes of toxic scarlet
berries in early summer.
◨ ◪ ◊ ✳✳✳
A. italicum 'Marmoratum' ♀
p.40.

Aruncus dioicus ♀
(Goat's beard)
Tall perennial grown for its
divided, fern-like leaves and
pyramidal sprays of creamy-
white flowers, borne in
summer. A moisture-loving
plant that suits damp borders
or woodland plantings.
◨ ◪ ❋ ◊ ✳✳✳

Asarum hartwegii
(Wild ginger)
Small, evergreen, ground-
cover perennial with dark
green leaves that are marbled
silver-green. Tiny, urn-shaped
flowers appear in late spring
and early summer. For border
edges and beneath shrubs.
◨ ◪ ❋ ◊ ✳✳✳

Asplenium
Medium, evergreen and semi-
evergreen, upright ferns which
form shuttlecocks of bright
green, leathery fronds, often
with wavy or ruffled margins.
◨ ◪ ❋ ◊ ✳✳✳
A. scolopendrium Crispum
Group *p.44*.

Astilbe
Small, clump-forming
perennials with divided leaves
and plumes of tiny white,
red or pink flowers, borne
during late spring or summer.
For damp borders and
woodland plantings.
◨ ◪ ◊ ✳✳✳
A. 'Irrlicht' *p.40*.

AQUILEGIA VULGARIS 'NIVEA' | *ASTILBE* 'FANAL'

Astrantia (Masterwort)
Medium, clump-forming
perennials bearing tiny
flowers with papery, pink or
white bracts in summer. For
damp borders or streamsides.
🔲 🔲 ◊ ◊ ✻✻✻
A. major 'Shaggy' ♀ *p.40*.

Athyrium (Lady fern)
Small, elegant, deciduous
ferns with arching fronds.
A. niponicum 'Pictum' has
silver-grey segments with
maroon stalks and midribs.
For borders and woodland.
🔲 🔲 ◊ ✻✻✻
A. niponicum 'Pictum' ♀
p.44.

Aucuba japonica
Tall, evergreen shrub with
bold, often variegated leaves
and large fruits. Valued for its
tolerance of poor soils, deep
shade and pollution. Use as
hedging or in shrub borders.
🔲 🔲 ✳ ◊ ◊ ✻✻✻
Recommended:
'Crotonifolia' ♀.

B

Bergenia (Elephant's ears)
Small, low-growing, evergreen
perennials grown for their
foliage and pink or white
flowers in late winter and
early spring. For border
edges and woodland gardens.
🔲 🔲 ◊ ✻✻✻
Bergenia purpurascens p.34.

Betula (Birch)
Deciduous trees with
an airy branch structure
and beautiful bark. Use as
specimens or in woodland.
🔲 🔲 ◊ ✻✻✻
B. ermanii 'Grayswood
Hill' ♀ *p.40*.

CALLICARPA BODINIERI VAR.
GIRALDII 'PROFUSION'

Blechnum (Hard fern)
Small to medium, evergreen,
creeping ferns with leathery,
dark green fronds. Suitable
as ground cover in damp
borders, woodland gardens
and ferneries.
🔲 🔲 ▣ ◊ ᵉ ✻✻✻
Recommended: *B. chilense*, *B.
penna-marina*, *B. spicant* ♀.

Brunnera macrophylla
Small perennial bearing rich
blue, forget-me-not-like
flowers in spring. Bright green
leaves expand after flowering
to create good ground cover.
Needs shelter from dry winds.
🔲 🔲 ◊ ✻✻✻
B. macrophylla ♀ *p.40* and
'Dawson's White' *p.26*.
Also recommended: 'Hadspen
Cream' ♀.

Buxus (Box)
Medium, evergreen, small-
leaved shrubs of rounded
habit. Tolerate clipping and
suit hedging or topiary;
dwarf cultivars can be used
as edging or in containers.
🔲 🔲 ◊ ✻✻✻
B. sempervirens 'Suffruticosa'
♀ *p.30*.

CAMPANULA LACTIFLORA
'LODDON ANNA'

C

Callicarpa bodinieri
(Beauty berry)
Tall, deciduous shrub with
small, pink summer flowers
and bead-like, violet fruits in
autumn, borne freely if grown
in groups. For shrub borders.
🔲 ◊ ✻✻✻

Camellia × *williamsii*
Tall, elegant, evergreen shrubs
or small trees with glossy,
dark green foliage and showy
pink, red, white or yellow
flowers borne from mid-
winter to early spring.
Suitable as specimen plants
or for borders and woodland.
🔲 🔲 ◊ ᵉ ✻✻✻

Campanula (Bellflower)
Medium to tall herbaceous
perennials valued for their
nodding, bell-shaped flowers,
in shades of blue or pink,
borne in summer. For lightly
shaded borders or open
woodland gardens.
🔲 🔲 ◊ ✻✻✻
C. persicifolia 'Telham Beauty'
p.34.

CAREX OSHIMENSIS 'EVERGOLD'

Carex (Sedge)
Medium tufts of evergreen grass-like leaves, several with golden foliage. Brown flower spikelets appear in summer. Suitable for gravel gardens. *C. hachijoensis* suits containers.
🔲 🔳 ◊ ✳✳✳
C. elata 'Aurea' ♀ *p.44.*

Celastrus orbiculatus
(Bittersweet, Staff vine)
Tall, vigorous, twining climber with scalloped or toothed, mid-green leaves and small green flowers in summer. Grown for its yellow fruits in autumn, which split open to reveal coloured seeds. For pergolas, fences or walls.
🔲 🔳 ◊ ◊ ✳✳✳

Chaenomeles (Japanese quince, Japonica)
Tall, deciduous, often spiny, shrubs grown for their white, red or pink cup-shaped spring flowers, followed by edible, purplish-green fruits. Good against shady walls.
🔲 🔳 ◊ ◊ ✳✳✳
Recommended: *C. × superba* 'Crimson and Gold' ♀ and 'Pink Lady' ♀.

Chelidonium majus (Greater celandine)
Medium, clump-forming perennial valued for its deeply divided leaves and yellow, cup-shaped flowers (double in 'Flore Pleno') in summer. For woodland or wild gardens.
🔲 🔳 ▦ ◊ ◊ ✳✳✳

Chionodoxa forbesii
(Glory of the snow)
Small bulb with spreading, bright green leaves and blue, star-shaped flowers in early spring. For underplanting.
🔳 ◊ ✳✳✳

Choisya ternata ♀ (Mexican orange blossom)
Tall, evergreen shrub grown for its glossy leaves and scented white flowers, borne in spring and summer. For courtyards and borders.
🔲 🔳 ◊ ✳✳✳

Cimicifuga racemosa ♀
(Bugbane)
Tall, clump-forming perennial bearing tiny white flowers in summer. For woodland gardens or borders.
🔲 🔳 ◊ ✳✳✳

CHAENOMELES SPECIOSA 'MOERLOOSEI'

CLEMATIS 'NELLY MOSER'

Clematis (Old man's beard)
Tall, evergreen and deciduous climbers grown for their mass of showy flowers, which are often followed by decorative seedheads. For training into host plants or on walls.
🔲 🔳 ◊ ✳✳✳
C. 'Alba Luxurians' ♀ *p.30;*
C. rehderiana ♀ *p.30.*

Clethra alnifolia
(Summer sweet)
Tall, clump-forming shrub with spikes of fragrant white flowers in late summer. For woodland or borders.
🔲 🔳 ◊ ◊ ✳✳✳

Convallaria
(Lily-of-the-valley)
Small, herbaceous perennials with sprays of scented, waxy-white flowers. Suitable for ground cover under trees. Can be invasive.
🔲 🔳 ▦ ◊ ✳✳✳

Cornus mas ♀
Tall, vigorous, deciduous shrub distinguished by its yellow blooms borne on bare branches in late winter. For woodland gardens.
🔲 🔳 ◊ ✳✳✳

COTONEASTER
'ROTHSCHILDIANUS'

Corydalis lutea
Small perennial grown for its fern-like foliage and spurred yellow flowers from late spring to autumn. For woodland or borders.
🔲 🔲 ◊ ◊ ✱✱✱

Corylopsis pauciflora ♀
Tall, deciduous shrub bearing drooping, bell-shaped, pale yellow flowers on bare branches in spring. For shrub borders or woodland gardens.
🔲 🔲 ◊ ◊ ✱✱✱

Corylus maxima (Filbert)
Tall, deciduous shrub grown for its foliage, spring catkins and edible nuts. For borders or as informal hedging.
🔲 🔲 ▩ ◊ ◊ ✱✱✱

Cotoneaster
Ranging in height from small to tall, deciduous or evergreen shrubs and trees grown for their foliage, spring flowers and autumn berries. Good for informal screens, shrub borders and woodland gardens.
🔲 🔲 ◊ ✱✱✱

Cyclamen hederifolium ♀
(Sowbread)
Small perennial with nodding, pink or white flowers in autumn, followed by mats of dark green leaves with silver marbling. Underplant beneath shrubs or conifers. Tolerates dry soils.
🔲 🔲 ◊ ✱✱✱
Recommended: 'Albiflorum'.

D

Danae racemosa ♀
(Alexandrian laurel)
Medium, clump-forming, evergreen perennial grown for its slender shoots and glossy leaves. Spikes of tiny, yellow-green flowers are borne in early summer, followed by glossy, bright red berries in autumn. For woodland gardens or shrub groupings.
🔲 🔲 ◊ ✱✱✱

Dicentra
Small to medium perennials valued for their fern-like leaves and sprays of drooping, heart-shaped flowers, in white, yellow, pink or red, produced in spring and summer. For borders or woodland gardens.
🔲 🔲 ◊ ◊ ✱✱✱
D. spectabilis 'Alba' ♀ p.34.
Also recommended:
D. 'Bacchanal', D. 'Pearl Drops', D. spectabilis ♀.

Digitalis purpurea
(Foxglove)
Tall biennial or short-lived perennial noted for its spires of bell-shaped flowers borne in summer. For mixed or herbaceous borders. Suits naturalizing in woodland.
🔲 🔲 ◊ ✱✱✱

Dryopteris erythrosora ♀
(Buckler fern)
Medium, deciduous fern with shuttlecocks of arching fronds. For wild or woodland gardens and ferneries.
🔲 🔲 ▩ ◊ ✱✱✱

E

Enkianthus campanulatus ♀
Tall, deciduous shrub valued for its small, urn-shaped, white, cream or red flowers borne in spring and early summer, followed by colourful leaves in autumn. For borders or woodland.
🔲 🔲 ◊ ✱✱✱

Epimedium grandiflorum ♀
(Barrenwort)
Small, clump-forming perennial grown for its heart-shaped leaves that are colourful when young and in autumn. Spurred, cup- or saucer-shaped flowers appear in spring and early summer. For woodland or borders.
🔲 🔲 ◊ ✱✱✱
Recommended: 'Crimson Beauty' and 'Rose Queen' ♀.

ENKIANTHUS
CAMPANULATUS

EUONYMUS FORTUNEI
'SILVER QUEEN'

Eranthis hyemalis ♀
(Winter aconite)
Small perennial grown for its cup-shaped yellow flowers with distinctive, bright green ruffs, borne in late winter or early spring. Use among shrubs and trees or naturalize in fine grass.

▦ ▨ ◊ ◊ ✳✳✳

Erythronium
(Dog's-tooth violet)
Small, clump-forming perennials grown for their drooping spring flowers, in shades of white, yellow, pink or purple. For underplanting trees and shrubs.

▦ ▨ ◊ ✳✳✳

Recommended: *E. californicum* 'White Beauty' ♀, *E. oreganum, E. revolutum* ♀.

Euonymus fortunei
Small to medium, mound-forming shrub, valued for its white- or golden-variegated foliage. For ground cover in borders. May be allowed to scramble through trees.

▦ ▨ ◊ ◊ ✳✳✳

Recommended: 'Emerald 'n' Gold' ♀.

FOTHERGILLA MAJOR

Euphorbia (Spurge)
Annuals and perennials that vary in size, most with eye-catching yellow-green, or sometimes flame-coloured heads of bracts in spring and summer. Tolerate deep shade and dry soils. Will self-sow.

▨ ▦ ▨ ◊ ◊ ✳✳✳

E. characias subsp. *wulfenii* ♀ p.26. Also recommended: *E. amygdaloides* var. *robbiae* ♀.

F

Fargesia
Tall, evergreen, clump-forming bamboos with bright green leaves contrasted against yellow or purple-brown stems. For borders and woodland gardens.

▦ ▨ ◊ ✳✳✳

Recommended: *F. murieliae* ♀, *F. nitida* ♀.

x Fatshedera lizei ♀
Tall, evergreen shrub with large sprays of cream flowers borne in autumn. Tie in against shady walls in courtyards and borders.

▦ ▨ ◊ ◊ ✳✳

Fothergilla major ♀
Tall, deciduous shrub with scented, white bottlebrush flowers in spring and early summer, and brilliant autumn colour. Suitable for borders and woodland gardens.

▦ ▨ ◊ ◊ ✳✳✳

G

Galanthus nivalis ♀
(Snowdrop)
Small, bulbous perennial grown for its drooping, white, pear-shaped flowers, borne in late winter and spring. For underplanting beneath shrubs in borders, or naturalizing in grass or woodland.

▦ ▨ ▦ ◊ ✳✳✳

Recommended: 'Flore Pleno' ♀.

Galium odoratum
(Sweet woodruff)
Small, low-growing, spreading perennial with slender leaves and tiny, scented, star-shaped white flowers produced from spring to summer. Ground cover for woodland gardens or beneath shrubs in borders.

▦ ▨ ◊ ◊ ✳✳✳

GALIUM ODORATUM

Garrya elliptica
Tall, evergreen shrub or small tree bearing long, silver-grey catkins from mid-winter to spring. For shady walls and borders.
◧ ▨ ◊ ◑ ✳✳
Recommended: 'James Roof' ♀.

Gaultheria mucronata
Medium, evergreen shrub valued for its glossy dark green foliage, urn-shaped white flowers and large, showy pink, crimson or white fruits. For woodland gardens.
◧ ▨ ◊ ♨ ✳✳✳
Recommended: 'Mulberry Wine' ♀ and 'Wintertime' ♀.

Gentiana asclepiadea
(Willow gentian)
Medium perennial noted for its rich blue, trumpet-shaped blooms (see p.36), borne in spring and autumn. For shady borders and woodland gardens. May naturalize in ideal conditions.
◧ ▨ ◊ ♨ ✳✳✳

Geranium (Cranesbill)
Small to medium perennials valued for their lobed, often aromatic leaves and saucer-shaped flowers in shades of white, pink, purple or blue. Suitable as ground cover beneath shrubs, in borders or woodland gardens.
◧ ▨ ◊ ◊ ✳✳✳
G. phaeum and 'Album' p.30.

Gymnocarpium dryopteris ♀
Small, deciduous, ground-covering fern noted for its distinctive triangular fronds. For borders, ferneries and woodland gardens.
◧ ▨ ◊ ✳✳✳

H

Hakonechloa
Small, clump-forming perennial grass valued for its reddish autumn tints. For shady borders or woodland.
◧ ▨ ◊ ◊ ✳✳✳
H. macra 'Aureola' ♀ p.36.

Halesia carolina (Silver bell)
Deciduous tree with white, bell-shaped flowers in spring or early summer, and colourful autumn foliage. For woodland or shrub borders.
◧ ▨ ◊ ◊ ✳✳✳

Hamamelis (Witch hazel)
Tall, deciduous shrubs valued for their autumn colour and scented, yellow, spidery flowers in winter or early spring.
◧ ▨ ◊ ◊ ✳✳✳

Hedera (Ivy)
Evergreen climbers, often with coloured or variegated leaves. For walls and ground cover. Tolerate dry shade.
◧ ▨ ◊ ♨ ✳✳✳
H. helix 'Buttercup' p. 26;
H. helix 'Glacier' ♀ p.40.

HEDERA HELIX 'PEDATA'

HEPATICA NOBILIS 'JAPONICA'

Helleborus (Hellebore)
Small, clump-forming, sometimes evergreen perennials with lobed or divided leaves, and saucer-shaped flowers in white and shades of cream, pink, green or purple, borne from late winter to spring. For shrub or mixed borders. May be naturalized in woodland.
◧ ▨ ◊ ✳✳✳
H. niger 'Potter's Wheel' p.40;
H. x hybridus 'Ballard's Black' p.40.

Hepatica nobilis
Small, semi-evergreen, clump-forming perennial with bowl-shaped white, pink or blue flowers borne in early spring. For border edges and woodland gardens.
◧ ▨ ◊ ✳✳✳

Heuchera (Coral flower)
Small, fully or semi-evergreen perennials bearing spikes of tiny pink, red or greenish flowers in spring and summer. Use as ground cover in borders or woodland gardens.
◧ ▨ ▦ ◊ ◊ ✳✳✳
H. 'Pewter Moon' p.40. Also recommended: H. cylindrica.

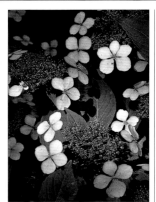

HYDRANGEA SERRATA 'BLUEBIRD'

Hosta

Small to medium perennials valued for their foliage, with mauve flowers borne above the leaves in mid- to late summer. For damp sites.
◨ ◪ ▣ ◊ ✳✳✳
'Albomarginata' *p.44*; 'Birchwood Parky's Gold' *p.26*; 'Frances Williams' ♥ *p.30*; 'Gold Standard' *p.26*.

Hyacinthoides hispanica

(Spanish bluebell)
Small, bulbous perennial bearing nodding, bell-shaped, blue flowers in spring. For underplanting in woodland gardens or shrub borders.
◨ ◪ ◊ ✳✳✳

Hydrangea

Medium to tall shrubs and one self-clinging climber, *H. anomala*, grown for their lacecap or mop-head flower-heads, in white and shades of pink or blue, in late summer. For borders or woodland.
◨ ◪ ◊ ✳✳✳
H. paniculata 'Grandiflora' ♥ *p.36*; *H. anomala* subsp. *petiolaris* ♥ *p.40*; *H. quercifolia* ♥ *p.30*.

Hypericum (St John's wort)

Medium evergreen, semi-evergreen and deciduous shrubs valued for their showy yellow flowers. Those recommended tolerate poor, dry soils and make good ground cover.
◨ ◪ ▣ ◊ ◊ ✳✳✳
Recommended: *H. andro-saemum*, *H. calycinum*.

I

Ilex (Holly)

Tall, mostly evergreen shrubs and small trees with colourful winter-persistent fruits and glossy foliage. Cultivars variegated with cream, white or gold need more light than green-leaved forms. May be clipped.
◨ ◪ ◊ ◊ ✳✳✳
Recommended:
I. × meserveae, *I. opaca*.

Impatiens (Busy Lizzie)

Small bedding plants that produce brightly coloured flowers throughout summer. For borders and containers.
◨ ◪ ◊ Min. 5°C

HYPERICUM ANDROSAEMUM 'ALBURY PURPLE'

Iris sibirica (Siberian flag)

Medium-height, beardless iris with narrow, grass-like leaves and dark-veined blue or blue-purple flowers, borne in early summer. For watersides and borders.
◪ ◊ ✳✳✳
'Lady of Quality' *p.34*. Also recommended: 'Alba' ♥.

Itea virginica (Sweetspire, Tassel-white)

Tall, deciduous shrub with colourful autumn foliage and upright spikes of fragrant, creamy-white flowers, borne in summer. For shrub borders or open glades in woodland.
◨ ◪ ◊ ◊ ✳✳✳

J

Jasminum nudiflorum ♥

(Winter jasmine)
Tall, slender, deciduous shrub valued for its bright yellow flowers produced on bare stems in winter and early spring. Needs support when grown as a climber. For pergolas, arbours or walls.
◨ ◪ ◊ ◊ ✳✳

ILEX AQUIFOLIUM 'ARGENTEA MARGINATA'

Jeffersonia dubia (Twin leaf)
Small perennial grown for its lobed leaves and cup-shaped, white or lavender flowers, borne on long, slender stalks in late spring and early summer. Suitable for damp sites.
🔲 🔲 ⬛ ◊ ✻✻✻

K

Kirengeshoma palmata ♀
Medium to tall perennial with sycamore-like leaves and waxy, pale yellow flowers in late summer and autumn. For woodland gardens or borders.
🔲 🔲 ◊ ♨ ✻✻✻

L

Lamium (Dead nettle)
Small, spreading perennials with wrinkled, often marked leaves and small, pink or white flowers from early spring to summer. Good ground cover.
🔲 🔲 ⬛ ◊◊ ✻✻✻
L. maculatum 'Beacon Silver' *p.40.*

*KIRENGESHOMA
PALMATA*

LAMIUM MACULATUM 'ALBUM'

Leucojum vernum ♀
(Spring snowflake)
Small, bulbous perennial valued for its nodding, bell-shaped white flowers in early and late spring. For woodland gardens and borders.
🔲 🔲 ◊ ✻✻✻

Leucothöe fontanesiana ♀
Tall, evergreen shrub with arching, zig-zag branches, glossy, dark green foliage and sprays of small, urn-shaped waxy-white flowers, borne in spring. For woodland.
🔲 🔲 ⬛ ◊ ♨ ✻✻✻

Leycesteria formosa ♀
Tall, thicket-forming, deciduous shrub with hanging spikes of tiny white flowers with purple bracts in summer and early autumn. For borders or woodland gardens.
🔲 🔲 ◊ ✻✻✻

Lilium (Lily)
Tall, elegant bulbous perennials with turkscap or trumpet-shaped flowers in summer. For containers in patios or courtyards.
🔲 🔲 ◊ ✻✻✻
L. martagon p.36.

Linnaea borealis
(Twin-flower)
Small, prostrate, evergreen shrub noted for its mats of glossy foliage and bell-shaped, pale pink flowers in summer. For woodland gardens.
🔲 🔲 ⬛ ◊ ♨ ✻✻✻

Liriope muscari ♀ (Lilyturf)
Evergreen perennial with narrow leaves and spikes of violet-mauve flowers in autumn. For ground cover.
🔲 🔲 ⬛ ◊◊ ♨ ✻✻✻

Lonicera (Honeysuckle)
Tall, evergreen or deciduous, twining climbers valued for their often scented summer flowers, in shades of yellow, pink or red. For arbours, walls or through trees.
🔲 🔲 ◊◊ ✻✻✻

Lunaria (Honesty)
Medium-height biennials and perennials with scented, white, violet or purple flowers in summer, followed by flat, silvery seedheads. For woodland gardens.
🔲 🔲 ◊◊ ✻✻✻
L. annua 'Variegata' *p.26.*

*LEYCESTERIA
FORMOSA*

LUZULA NIVEA

Luzula (Woodrush)
Small to medium, evergreen rushes forming clumps of flat leaves. The small flowers are ornamentally insignificant in most. Use as low ground cover in damp sites.
▨ ▨ ◊ ✳✳✳
Recommended: *L. sylvatica* 'Aurea' and 'Marginata'.

M

Mahonia aquifolium
(Oregon grape)
Small, evergreen shrub valued for its scented, yellow or orange flowers in spring. For ground cover in borders or woodland gardens.
▨ ▨ ✺ ◊ ◊ ✳✳✳
Recommended: 'Orange Flame' and 'Smaragd'.

Maianthemum bifolium
(May lily)
Small, ground-covering perennial grown for its glossy leaves and spikes of tiny, star-shaped white flowers, borne throughout spring. Suitable for wild gardens or woodland plantings.
▨ ▨ ✺ ◊ ᶜᵗ ✳✳✳

Matteuccia (Ostrich fern, Shuttlecock fern)
Tall, deciduous fern with arching, pale green fronds, followed by dark brown fertile fronds which form in the centre of the shuttlecock in late summer. For woodland gardens, shady borders, ferneries and at poolsides.
▨ ▨ ◊ ✳✳✳
M. struthiopteris ♥ *p.44.*

Meconopsis cambrica
(Welsh poppy)
Small perennial with deeply cut, blue-green leaves and poppy-like, yellow or orange flowers produced from spring to autumn. Suitable for woodland plantings, wild gardens and informal borders. Self-seeds freely.
▨ ▨ ◊ ✳✳✳
M. cambrica *pp.26 and 44.*

Myosotis sylvatica
(Forget-me-not)
Small biennial with yellow-eyed, rich blue or white flowers in spring and early summer. For woodland or wild gardens, or beneath shrubs in borders.
▨ ▨ ◊ ◊ ✳✳✳

MATTEUCCIA STRUTHIOPTERIS

N

Nicotiana (Tobacco plant)
Medium perennials valued for the range of subtle colours and scent of their trumpet-shaped flowers, borne for long periods during summer. For beds, borders or containers.
▨ ▨ ◊ ◊ ✳
N. sylvestris ♥ *p.36;*
N. 'Lime Green' ♥ *p.30.*

O

Omphalodes (Navelwort)
Small, evergreen perennials bearing forget-me-not-like, blue flowers in early spring. Suitable for ground cover in woodland gardens.
▨ ▨ ◊ ✳✳✳

Ornithogalum
(Star-of-Bethlehem)
Small bulbs grown for their starry white flowers, borne in spring or early summer. For shrub or mixed borders. May be naturalized in grass.
▨ ▨ ◊ ✳✳✳
Recommended: *O. nutans* ♥.

Osmanthus x **burkwoodii** ♥
Tall, dense, evergreen shrub bearing small clusters of tiny white, scented flowers in mid- to late spring, followed by blue-black berries. For large tubs, borders or hedging.
▨ ▨ ◊ ✳✳✳

Osmunda
Medium, deciduous ferns with triangular fronds which turn golden brown in autumn. For ferneries and watersides.
▨ ▨ ◊ ᶜᵗ ✳✳✳
O. cinnamomea ♥ *p.44.*

P

Pachyphragma macrophyllum

Small, mat-forming, semi-evergreen perennial valued for its clusters of tiny, white flowers, borne during early spring. For ground cover beneath trees and shrubs.
◧ ▧ ◊ ✱✱✱

Pachysandra

Small, fully or semi-evergreen, spreading perennials bearing coarsely toothed, dark green leaves and spikes of tiny white flowers in summer. Tolerates poor, dry soils. For ground cover.
◧ ▧ ✳ ◊ ◊ ✱✱✱
P. terminalis ♥ *p.40*. Also recommended: 'Variegata' ♥.

Parthenocissus henryana ♥

(Chinese Virginia creeper)
Tall, deciduous climber noted for its dark green, white-veined foliage, often pink-centred, and brilliant autumn colour. For training on walls or fences, or through trees.
◧ ▧ ◊ ◊ ✱✱✱

Phegopteris (Beech fern)

Small, attractive, carpet-forming fern with soft, pale green fronds. For woodland gardens, ferneries or damp, sheltered borders.
◧ ▧ ✳ ◊ 🜊 ✱✱✱
P. connectilis pp.36 and 44.

Photinia

Tall, compact evergreen shrub or tree grown for its foliage and clusters of small white flowers, borne in spring. For informal borders, woodland gardens or informal hedging.
◧ ▧ ◊ ✱✱✱

PHOTINIA x FRASERI 'RED ROBIN' ♥

Pieris japonica

Medium evergreen shrub with leathery, dark green leaves (bronze when young) and clusters of waxy-white flowers in late winter or spring. For shrub borders, woodland or large containers.
◧ ▧ ◊ 🜊 ✱✱✱

Podophyllum hexandrum

Small perennial bearing white or pink, cup-shaped flowers in spring and early summer. For woodland or damp borders. All parts are toxic.
◧ ▧ ✳ ◊ ✱✱✱

PODOPHYLLUM HEXANDRUM

POLEMONIUM PAUCIFLORUM 'PURPUREUS'

Polemonium (Jacob's ladder)

Small, clump-forming perennials with usually white or blue, bell-shaped flowers borne in spring and summer. For borders or wild garden. *P. caeruleum* may be naturalized in grass. Self-seeds freely.
◧ ▧ ◊ ◊ ✱✱✱
Recommended: *P. caeruleum*, *P.* 'Lambrook Mauve' ♥.

Polygonatum

(Solomon's seal)
Medium to tall, elegant perennials with bell-shaped, green-white flowers that hang from arching stems in spring or summer. For borders or woodland gardens.
◧ ▧ ✳ ◊ ✱✱✱
P. x hybridum ♥ p.34. Also recommended: *P. biflorum*.

Polypodium

Small, robust, evergreen ferns with arching, leathery fronds, some of which are crested or curled. For ground cover in ferneries, shady borders or woodland gardens.
◧ ▧ ✳ ◊ ✱✱✱
P. vulgare 'Cornubiense' ♥ *p.44*.

PYRACANTHA
'ORANGE GLOW' ♀

Polystichum (Holly fern)
Small to medium, evergreen ferns valued for their shuttlecocks of finely divided, fresh green fronds. Suitable for borders and ferneries or woodland gardens.
▨ ▨ ▩ ◊ ✳✳✳
P. setiferum Divisilobum Group ♀ *pp.34* and *44.*

Primula florindae
(Giant cowslip)
Medium, deciduous perennial grown for its toothed, mid-green leaves and slender, funnel-shaped, scented yellow flowers (see *p.34),* in summer. For informal plantings, damp borders, containers and woodland.
▨ ▨ ◊ ✳✳✳

Prunus laurocerasus ♀
(Cherry laurel)
Tall, compact, evergreen shrub valued for its spikes of white flowers borne in spring, followed by cherry-like red fruits in autumn. Tolerates pollution and most soil conditions.
▨ ▨ ▩ ◊ ◊ ✳✳✳
Recommended: 'Zabeliana'.

Pulmonaria (Lungwort)
Small perennials with funnel-shaped flowers, in white, blue, pink or purple, borne in late winter or early spring. For borders or woodland.
▨ ▨ ▩ ◊ ✳✳✳
P. 'Mawson's Blue' *p.40;*
P. officinalis 'Sissinghurst White' ♀ *p.40.*

Pyracantha (Firethorn)
Tall, spiny evergreen shrubs with white summer flowers and winter berries. For walls, mixed borders and hedging.
▨ ▨ ◊ ✳✳✳

R

Ranunculus aconitifolius
Small to medium, clump-forming perennial with white, saucer-shaped flowers in spring and early summer. For damp borders or woodland.
▨ ▨ ▩ ◊ ✳✳✳

Rheum palmatum ♀
Tall perennial with rhubarb-like leaves and spires of cream or dark red flowers in summer. For damp borders.
▨ ▨ ◊ ✳✳✳

RIBES ODORATUM

Rhododendron
Evergreen and deciduous shrubs and trees that range widely in height, grown for their impressive, sometimes scented spring flowers. For woodland and shrub borders.
▨ ▨ ◊ ⌖ ✳✳✳

Rhodotypos scandens
Tall, deciduous shrub with papery, white flowers in spring and summer, followed by shiny black berries. For woodland or shrub borders.
▨ ▨ ◊ ◊ ✳✳✳

Ribes (Flowering currants)
Medium, compact, deciduous shrubs grown for their clusters of bell-shaped pink, white or greenish-yellow flowers, borne in spring. For informal hedging and borders.
▨ ◊ ◊ ✳✳✳

Rodgersia pinnata
Tall, clump-forming perennial with crinkled lobed leaves, reddish-green stems, and spires of white, pink or red flowers, borne in late summer. For damp borders, watersides, and at woodland margins.
▨ ▩ ◊ ✳✳✳

RODGERSIA PINNATA 'SUPERBA'

ROSA 'NEW DAWN'

Rosa (Roses)
The Alba group of old roses is tall and tolerates shade. Many ramblers and climbers tolerate some shade on their lower halves, given good light on their top growth. For pergolas, arbours and walls.
▨ ▧ ◊ ✳✳✳
R. 'Albéric Barbier' ♀ *p.30;*
R. 'New Dawn' ♀ *p.30.*

Rubus tricolor
Medium, prostrate, evergreen shrub with glossy foliage, red-bristled shoots and cup-shaped white flowers borne in summer, followed by edible, red fruits in autumn. For ground cover in shrub borders.
▨ ▧ ▦ ◊ ✳✳✳

Ruscus (Broom)
Small to medium, shrubby evergreens with flattened, leaf-like shoots that bear tiny white, star-shaped flowers and glossy red fruits from late summer to winter. For dry borders.
▨ ▧ ▦ ◊ ✳✳✳
R. aculeatus *p.26.*
Also recommended:
R. hypoglossum.

S

Sambucus nigra
(Black elder)
Tall, deciduous shrub grown for its sprays of small, white to ivory flowers, followed by black, white or red fruits. Tolerates poor, dry or wet soils and pollution.
▨ ▧ ◊ ◊ ✳✳✳
Recommended: 'Aurea' ♀, 'Guincho Purple' and 'Laciniata' ♀.

Sanguinaria canadensis
(Bloodroot)
Small perennial with heart-shaped, blue-green, scalloped leaves and double white flowers in spring. For shrub and herbaceous borders.
▨ ▧ ▦ ◊ ✳✳✳
Recommended: 'Plena' ♀.

Sarcococca (Christmas box)
Medium, ground-covering, evergreen shrubs bearing fragrant, white or whitish-green flowers in winter. For shrub borders and dry soils.
▨ ▧ ▦ ◊ ✳✳✳
Recommended: S. hookeriana ♀, S. humilis, S. ruscifolia.

SAXIFRAGA GRANULATA

Saxifraga (Saxifrage)
Small, clump-forming, evergreen perennials with rosettes of leaves and small, white or pink, star- or cup-shaped flowers in spring. Suitable as ground cover even in poor soil. For borders and woodland gardens.
▨ ▧ ◊ ◊ ✳✳✳
Recommended: S. granulata 'Plena', S. × urbium (London pride).

Schizophragma integrifolium ♀
Tall, elegant, deciduous climber with long-stalked, dark green leaves and showy, white "lacecap" flowerheads, borne in summer. Suitable for training on walls, fences, pergolas and arbours, or through large trees.
▨ ▧ ◊ ◊ ✳✳✳

Scilla siberica ♀
(Siberian squill)
Small, bulbous perennials bearing nodding, bowl-shaped, bright blue flowers in spring. Good for underplanting among shrubs and trees. May be naturalized in woodland gardens.
▨ ▧ ◊ ◊ ✳✳✳

Shortia
Evergreen, ground-covering perennials valued for their rounded, dark green leaves which turn red in autumn, and funnel-shaped, white or deep pink flowers with deeply fringed petals, borne during spring. Suitable for damp borders or woodland plantings.
▨ ▧ ▦ ◊ ✳✳✳
Recommended: S. galacifolia, S. soldanelloides, S. uniflora 'Grandiflora'.

SKIMMIA JAPONICA
'BRONZE KNIGHT'

Skimmia japonica
Medium to tall, evergreen,
spring-flowering shrub valued
for its slightly aromatic leaves
and fragrant white flowers,
which open from red buds.
Tolerates pollution. For
containers, borders or
woodland gardens.
🌣 🌣 ☀ ◊ ◊ ✳✳✳
Recommended: 'Rubella' ♀.

Smilacina racemosa ♀
(False Solomon's seal)
Medium, clump-forming
perennial with unbranched,
often arching stems, bright
green foliage and dense
plumes of tiny cream flowers,
borne in spring. For damp
borders and woodland.
🌣 🌣 ☀ ◊ ✳✳✳

Sorbaria
Tall, deciduous shrubs valued
for their finely divided leaves
and sprays of white, star-like
flowers, produced from mid-
to late summer. For shrub
borders and woodland or
wild gardens.
🌣 🌣 ◊ ◊ ✳✳✳
S. tomentosa var. **angustifolia**
♀ p.40.

Stylophorum diphyllum
Small perennial grown for
its deeply cut leaves and
poppy-like, yellow flowers,
borne during summer. For
damp borders or may be
naturalized in woodland
gardens. May self-sow.
🌣 🌣 ☀ ◊ ✳✳✳

Styrax
Elegant, deciduous trees
noted for their fragrant, bell-
shaped white flowers, borne
in summer. Some have good
autumn colour. For sheltered
woodland gardens.
🌣 🌣 ◊ ◊ ✳✳✳
S. **japonicus** ♀ p.34. Also
recommended: S. **obassia** ♀.

Symphoricarpus
(Snowberry)
Tall, deciduous, thicket-
forming shrubs grown mainly
for their tiny, bell-shaped
flowers, which are highly
attractive to bees, and their
white, pink or dark blue,
winter-persistent fruits.
Tolerate pollution, poor soil
and exposure. For hedging
or screens.
🌣 🌣 ◊ ◊ ✳✳✳

STYLOPHORUM
DIPHYLLUM

TELLIMA GRANDIFLORA

T

Taxus baccata ♀ (Yew)
Tall, evergreen, coniferous
shrubs or trees valued for
their peeling, red-brown
bark, and dark green, needle-
like leaves and red, winter-
persistent fruits. Use as
specimens or for hedging.
🌣 🌣 ☀ ◊ ◊ ✳✳✳
Recommended: 'Dovastonii
Aurea' ♀.

Tellima grandiflora
(Fringe cup)
Small, rosette-forming
perennial with slender spikes
of green-white flowers in
spring and summer. Drought-
tolerant ground cover for
borders or woodland gardens.
🌣 🌣 ◊ ◊ ✳✳✳

Tiarella cordifolia ♀
(Foam flower)
Small, vigorous, ground-cover
perennial with heart-shaped
leaves, tinted bronze-red in
autumn, and upright spikes
of tiny cream flowers in
summer. For borders or
woodland gardens.
🌣 🌣 ◊ ◊ ✳✳✳

Tolmiea menziesii ♀
(Pick-a-back plant)
Small, dense, fast-spreading
perennial grown for its pale
green or yellow-green foliage
and small, greenish-purple
flowers, borne in late spring
and early summer. The leaves
of 'Taff's Gold' are spotted
and mottled cream and pale
yellow. For ground cover
beneath shrubs or trees.
▨ ▨ ▣ ◊ ◊ ✳✳✳
Recommended: 'Taff's
Gold' ♀.

Trachystemon orientale
Small to medium perennial
with heart-shaped leaves
and blue spring flowers.
For ground cover in wild
and woodland gardens.
▨ ▨ ◊ ◊ ✳✳✳

Tricyrtis (Toad lily)
Medium perennials with
prominently veined, pale
to dark green leaves and star-
or funnel-shaped, yellow- or
maroon-speckled flowers,
produced in spring, summer
or autumn. For woodland
gardens or borders.
▨ ▨ ▣ ◊ ✳✳✳
T. hirta p.36. Also
recommended: *T. formosana*
♀.

Trillium (Trinity flower)
Small perennials noted
for their net-veined leaves,
often with silver or purple
marbling, and nodding or
upright cup-shaped flowers
in shades of white, pink,
maroon or yellow, borne
during spring. For borders
or woodland plantings.
▨ ▨ ◊ ✳✳✳
Recommended:
T. grandiflorum ♀, *T. ovatum*,
T. rivale ♀, *T. sessile*.

U

Uvularia grandiflora ♀
(Large merrybells)
Small, elegant perennial with
nodding, yellow, bell-shaped
flowers in spring. For damp
borders or woodland gardens.
▨ ▨ ▣ ◊ ✳✳✳

V

Vancouveria
Small, ground-cover perennial
bearing airy sprays of spurred
white flowers in late spring.
For woodland gardens.
▨ ▨ ◊ ✳✳✳
V. hexandra p.36.

Viburnum
Tall, deciduous and evergreen
shrubs valued for their showy,
often fragrant flowers and
glossy fruits. Use as specimens
in shrub borders, woodland
gardens or large containers.
▨ ▨ ▣ ◊ ◊ ✳✳✳
Recommended: *V. burkwoodii*
'Park Farm Hybrid' ♀,
V. carlesii 'Aurora' ♀,
V. tinus 'Eve Price' ♀.

VIOLA RIVINIANA PURPUREA
GROUP

Vinca minor (Periwinkle)
Small, evergreen, ground-
covering shrub with dark
green leaves and white, blue,
blue-violet or pink flowers
from spring to autumn. For
woodland gardens, shady
banks and shrub borders.
▨ ▨ ▣ ◊ ◊ ✳✳✳

Viola odorata
Small, ground-covering
perennial with toothed, heart-
shaped leaves and sweetly
scented, white or blue-violet
flowers from late winter to
spring. For wild gardens or
woodland. Will self-sow.
▨ ▨ ◊ ✳✳✳
Also recommended:
V. riviniana.

W

Waldsteinia ternata
Small, spreading, semi-
evergreen perennial with
saucer-shaped, bright yellow
flowers borne in late spring
and early summer. For ground
cover beneath trees or at the
front of borders.
▨ ▨ ▣ ◊ ✳✳✳

WALDSTEINIA
TERNATA

INDEX

Page numbers in *italics* indicate illustrations

ACKNOWLEDGMENTS

Picture research Neale Chamberlain, Catherine Costelloe, Sam Ruston

Illustrations Gill Tomblin, Karen Cochrane

Index Hilary Bird

Dorling Kindersley would also like to thank: Susanne Mitchell, Karen Wilson and Barbara Haynes at the RHS, Vincent Square.

The Royal Horticultural Society
To learn more about the work of the Society, visit the RHS on the Internet at **www.rhs.org.uk**. Information includes news of events around the country, a horticultural database, international plant registers, results of plant trials and membership details.

Photography
The publisher would like to thank the following for their kind permission to reproduce the photographs:
(key: l=left, r=right, c=centre, b=bottom, t=top)

A-Z Botanical Collection: A Young 15tr, Christopher Knight 23tl, J Malcolm Smith 9tl
Garden Picture Library: Henk Dijkman 21tl, 24, John Miller 6, Roger Hyam 38, Steven Wooster 28
John Glover: 7bl, 15tl
Jerry Harpur: 12b, Philip Watson 11br
Andrew Lawson: 8b, 25bl, 29bl, Brook Cottage Alkerton 43bl, Designer: Wendy Lauderdale 32
Clive Nichols: White Windows, Hampshire 39bl
Photos Horticultural: 10br, 18b, 42
Harry Smith Collection: 9tr, 11tl, 13br
Elizabeth Whiting & Associates: 54

Jacket photography:
Garden Picture Library: Steven Wooster back tr; **Andrew Lawson:** back tc; **S&O Mathews Photography** back tl, front bl; **Photos Horticultural:** front r